Possessing Your Prophetic Promise

D0843649

by

Tim Bagwell

Unless otherwise indicated, all scripture references are from the Authorized King James Version of the Bible.

Scripture references marked "NIV" are from the New International Version of the Bible, Copyright © 1973, 1978, 1984 by International Bible Society, Colorado Springs, Colorado.

ISBN 1-884369-12-X

Published by:

The McDougal Publishing Company
PO Box 3595
Hagerstown, MD 21740-3595

Printed in the United States of America
For Worldwide Distribution

Contents

Introduction

Introduction

The mass exodus of the people of Israel from Egypt, their crossing of the Red Sea, and their travels in the wilderness for forty years have inspired Christians for centuries now. God was with them in such a real and visible way, sustaining them by daily miracles, leading them in supernatural ways, protecting them from the enemies they passed along the way, and even keeping their clothing from wearing out. What a mighty God we serve!

Many of us forget, however, that what began as such a great miracle in Egypt ended in personal tragedy for an entire generation in the wilderness. One by one, the Israelites died in the desert without ever seeing the Promised Land, much less having possessed it. They had come so far, but not quite far enough. They had learned so much, but not quite enough.

In many ways, this tragedy of the wilderness reminds me of the state of the Church today. We have come so far, and we have learned so much. We have seen the hand of God, and we have witnessed His miracles. Still, the fullness of what God has promised us, as individuals, as families, and as a Church, is largely unfulfilled and yet lies as a hazy dream somewhere out ahead of us.

What must we do to cross over Jordan and possess our Promised Land? What steps are necessary to dislodge every enemy and take back what is rightfully ours? What must I do, personally? What must you do, personally? Come with me as we explore God's revelation for *Possessing Your Prophetic Promise.*

Tim Bagwell
Denver, Colorado

Chapter 1

Out of Egypt

And Moses spake so unto the children of Israel: but they hearkened not unto Moses for anguish of spirit, and for cruel bondage. Exodus 6:9

God gave Moses the prophetic word for his day, and Moses knew that it was time to lead God's children out of bondage and into their Promised Land. And he tried to tell the people, but they wouldn't listen to him.

Most of us can understand that. We have family or friends to whom we talk about God, but they ridicule us, laugh at us, or just ignore us — until we sometimes get very frustrated. *Why do they refuse to hear what God is saying?* we wonder. Their reluctance is hard for us to understand.

God says in His Word that because of their *"anguish of spirit and cruel bondage"* the children of Israel didn't listen to Moses. Some people have been oppressed and in bondage for so long that they simply can't understand how things could be different. When we talk to them about the salvation of the Lord, we might as well be speaking Greek. They can't comprehend it. They can't imagine what it would be like to have the joy of the Lord. They can't understand what it would feel like to be free. Their minds have been set by their circumstances. They have a defeatist mentality. They are sure they will always be bound, always be sick, and always be poor. And it's hard to convince them otherwise.

The children of Israel couldn't envision themselves in any other context than as slaves in Egypt. They had been slaves so long — ever since they could remember — that they knew no other way of life. When God's time had come to set them free and send them on their way toward their promised land, they found it difficult to accept that deliverance. They were bound by a slave mentality.

God, however, was not frustrated with these people, as we might have been. He didn't tell Moses what we might have told him, "All right, Moses, forget it. If these people want to be slaves, then let them be slaves. What do you expect me to do?"

No! God is a good and merciful God. He always wants the very best for His people, and He is very patient in leading us into His will for our lives.

God told Moses to go and speak to Pharaoh about setting the people of Israel free:

> *And the* LORD *spake unto Moses, saying, Go in, speak unto Pharaoh king of Egypt, that he let the children of Israel go out of his land.*
> Exodus 6:10-11

So, because God chose Him, Moses became God's man, whether the people accepted him or not; and he became the deliverer of the people, whether they liked it or not. Rejected by the Israelites, but chosen of God, Moses stood alone to do battle with the powerful Pharaoh, a battle for the souls of his people.

This battle was ordained of God and had nothing to do with whether or not Israel believed that Moses was to be their deliverer. God's ambassador faced the leader of the Egyptian Empire. Egypt is a type of the world, so God's man squared off against the enemy's man. This was a classic battle between the Spirit of God and the spirit of hell.

When will we realize that we are not dealing with personalities or with people's flesh? The Scriptures say it clearly:

> *For we wrestle not against flesh and blood, but against principalities, against powers, against*

the rulers of the darkness of this world, against
spiritual wickedness in high places.

Ephesians 6:12

We are facing the spiritual Pharaoh, the evil prince who rules over the lives of men. God has chosen us, as He did Moses, to receive His power and to utilize it against the powers that bind our loved ones, our neighbors, our schools, our cities, and our nations. The people we are sent to deliver may not be willing or able to recognize that God is using us for their deliverance, but that doesn't matter. We are not alone. Go forth against the pharaohs of this present world with faith that God will keep His word, whatever men may do or say.

Moses had no army. He had no bodyguards to accompany him into the presence of Pharaoh. He was one man against an empire. But that one man had a mission from God, and he dared not fail. Moses walked boldly into Pharaoh's throne room, looked the ruler in the eye, and said, "God said to let His people go."

There were no troops waiting outside ready to fight for him. His "troops" were in the brick pits, slaving under the lash of Pharaoh's overlords, unable or unwilling to come to his aid. He was alone with God.

Was Moses afraid? No! He knew that he had authority over anything or anyone who was holding God's people in captivity; and when, at first, Pharaoh refused his request, the power of God was demonstrated through Moses to convince the man.

It took a while; but after several demonstrations of God's power, Pharaoh let the people go.

We are destined for victory, and we must not give up until victory comes. God wants us to rise up in demonstration of His power and take authority over principalities, powers, rulers of the darkness of this world, and spiritual wickedness in high places. Only then will the devil loose his hold on people.

Too many Christians today are trying to sign peace treaties with the devil. They're looking for compromises and embracing philosophies that won't offend anybody. But that changes nothing and gets us nowhere. This is not a battle between flesh and flesh. This is a battle between spirit and spirit:

> *For though we walk in the flesh, we do not war*
> *after the flesh:*   2 Corinthians 10:3

Satan is exerting every effort to control as many people as he can. He knows that there is a war going on, and he is maneuvering and manipulating whomever he can to accomplish his purpose. He is trying to influence us through people we know or meet, through the books we read, and especially through the television programs we watch.

God said:

> *Wherein in time past ye walked according to the*
> *course of this world, according to the prince of*
> *the power of the air, the spirit that now worketh*
> *in the children of disobedience:*
>   Ephesians 2:2

That is not to say that everyone who doesn't go to church is demon possessed, but certainly they are under the influence of the enemy. And he is determined to extend his influence to our lives, as well. As Christians, we are under the influence of the Holy Ghost, although the degree to which we allow Him to guide us is a matter of our will and personal choice. But the devil is trying every way he can to get us to stray to the right or to the left. He is pulling at us in every direction. If we are to survive the onslaught of the enemy, we must submit ourselves to the Holy Spirit in this hour and be constantly led by Him. He is able to take us through that *"valley of the shadow of death"* and cause us to say, like David, *"I will fear no evil"* (Psalms 23:4).

Moses walked into Pharaoh's throne room without fear because he knew the authority he had in God. Do you know your authority in God? You may be one of those who sit back and think, "There's nothing I can do. This thing is out of control." But that is a lie of the enemy. Things are not out of control. We are serving the same God that Moses served; and we have the same call that he had: to loose our children, our spouses, our parents, our brothers and sisters, and our neighbors from the power of the enemy.

Satan will not give them up without a fight. When Daniel decided to fast and pray for his people, he found that it was not as easy as he might have imagined. He prayed and fasted for three weeks without any apparent results. At the end of the time, however, an angel of the Lord appeared to him and spoke to him:

> *Then said he unto me, Fear not, Daniel: for from the first day that thou didst set thine heart to understand, and to chasten thyself before thy God, thy words were heard, and I am come for thy words. But the prince of the kingdom of Persia withstood me one and twenty days: but, lo, Michael, one of the chief princes, came to help me; and I remained there with the kings of Persia.* Daniel 10:12-13

God was determined to get His message through to Daniel, and He's just as determined to get His message through to us. The angel of the Lord had been doing battle with the principality of the air that ruled over Persia. This satanic force was preventing the angel from bringing God's message to Daniel; but the archangel Michael was dispatched to help the angel, and together they won the battle:

> *Now I am come to make thee understand what shall befall thy people in the latter days: for yet the vision is for many days.* Daniel 10:14

God had a prophetic message for the people of Daniel's day, and the enemy did everything in his power to stop that message from being received. This doesn't surprise me at all. I see it happening today, as well. God has a prophetic message for our day. He is sending His message to the prophets; but at the same time, the devil is doing everything he can to prevent that message from arriving.

We can't just sit back and hope that the message gets here. No! We must get on our faces before God in serious fasting and prayer and intercession, as Daniel did. That is exactly what a remnant of God's people all over the world are doing today. They are seeking God seriously, staying in tune with His Spirit, and decreeing in unison the things God is speaking to them as His will for our day.

This is not a time for discouragement. It is not a time to dwell on the evil things that are happening around us. It is time to rise up and bring deliverance to those who are bound. It is time to move out of Egypt's sphere of influence and start marching toward the Promised Land.

This effort takes serious commitment. Mere rhetoric will not get the job done. When you stand against Satan's power, you must know what you are doing. The example of the sons of Sceva, in early New Testament times, shows that fact clearly:

> *Then certain of the vagabond Jews, exorcists, took upon them to call over them which had evil spirits the name of the Lord Jesus, saying, We adjure you by Jesus whom Paul preacheth. And there were seven sons of one Sceva, a Jew, and chief of the priests, which did so. And the evil spirit answered and said, Jesus I know, and Paul I know; but who are ye? And the man in whom the evil spirit was leaped on them, and overcame*

*them, and prevailed against them, so that they
fled out of that house naked and wounded.*
Acts 19:13-16

Those who fight this enemy must be known and
recognized as being on God's side. They must have a
personal relationship with the God under Whose
banner they go out to fight, and they must be in tune
with what He is saying to His Church today. If not,
they will surely be defeated.

You can't show fear for a moment, or the enemy
will take advantage of you every time. When we see
the evils that are coming into the Church and see
fellow ministers and believers being caught up in
scandals, it would be easy to draw the conclusion
that these things will surely "put a wet blanket" on
the move of the Spirit that we are seeing. But when
we are tempted to despair, we must remind ourselves of the lives of the early believers. The Church
of the Book of Acts had no Christian books, no Christian television, and no cassette tapes; yet every time
it underwent persecution, it grew. In the space of two
and a half years, the laborers of the first century
church were able to reach all of Asia for God (see
Acts 19:10). Those believers were not just surviving;
they were moving forward to possess their Promised
Land.

Satan never gave up on the early church but came
against it with every weapon he could muster. Those
saints had done nothing wrong; yet they were
burned at the stake, skinned alive, boiled in oil, and
served up as entrees to hungry lions. There is noth-

ing "normal" about that kind of behavior; it is clearly influenced by Satan himself. When the enemy sees his strongholds about to topple, he uses every tactic he can to stop the people of God. He comes against us with methods which can cause fear and intimidation. But fearful people are not possessors; they become, instead, passive survivors.

This is not a time to slow down or back off or give up. This is not a time to maintain a low profile or to move back from the front lines in fear of being shot at. Don't give Satan the satisfaction of forcing you to the sidelines. The order of the day is FORWARD, people of God. We are destined to victory.

Don't worry about the outcome. Jesus said:

> *He that findeth his life shall lose it: and he that loseth his life for my sake shall find it.*
> Matthew 10:39

Thank God there is a remnant of people today who are ready to rise up in His power and say:

> "I will not compromise. I am willing to lose my life for the Lord's sake because I am confident that He will save me, whatever else happens. I refuse to sit back in my comfortable position, but will go forth to pursue the enemy. I am ready to face the pharaohs of our time, to press forward to bring liberty to those who are in bondage from Egypt, and to move forward toward possessing my prophetic promise."

Chapter 2

Wandering in the Wilderness

For in him we live, and move, and have our being. Acts 17:28

The Exodus was precipitated by the blood of the Passover. Each of the plagues of Egypt represented the demolishing of an Egyptian god, but none of the early plagues resulted in deliverance for the people of Israel. The false gods of Egypt had to be humbled; for God recognized the lack of spiritual maturity in His people and knew that if the Egyptian gods were not destroyed, the people of Israel might, at some point, revert to worshiping them. To possess their heritage, they had to step into a new spiritual level.

They were delivered from Egypt through signs and wonders. They miraculously crossed the Red Sea and witnessed the destruction of Pharaoh's army in its waters. They drank water from the rock and ate manna from heaven.

During forty years of wandering, their clothes and shoes never wore out. They were delivered from the enemy bands who would have done them harm as they passed through the land. They received the Ten Commandments on Mt. Sinai and witnessed the special manifestation of God's presence through the wilderness Tabernacle. On the day of its dedication, the glory of God came down in such a way that the priests could not stand in the presence of God.

Despite the miracles, and despite the presence of the glory of God with them, Moses and the other members of his generation who witnessed the plagues in Egypt and partook of the first Passover supper never reached the Promised Land. With all that God had provided for them and with all they had witnessed, nevertheless, Moses' generation represents failure to possess. They turned into a generation of maintenance, not of possession. True, they maintained their faith in God for forty years, and that is laudable; but it was not enough. They maintained what they had, but they did not press on into the greater thing that was waiting for them on the other side of Jordan. They died in the wilderness without ever having possessed their prophetic promise. **Why?** This is a most important question, especially to those of us who have received a great prophetic promise from God. If we can discover the reasons behind Israel's failure, that may shed light on our own failures and, hopefully, help to prevent them in the future.

After the Exodus from Egypt, God purposely took His people through the wilderness. This was not for the sake of judgment, as many might suppose, but it was to preparation them to possess all that God had prepared for them.

This preparation would not be easy, for He was dealing with a group of people who had been stripped of their dignity, stripped of their heritage, and stripped of the revelation of who they were in God. In order to move in and possess their birthright, they had to experience a restoration of the revelation of what it meant to be the people of God.

As they moved into the wilderness, God began to teach them that IN HIM they would *live and move and have [their] being*. He taught them by providing manna to feed them, a cloud to cover them and protect them from the sun by day, and a fire to warm them by night. When they needed water, He brought it out of a rock. He sweetened the poisoned waters at Marah. During the forty years of their wandering in the wilderness, their clothes and shoes never wore out. All of this happened, not just as an act of God's mercy upon a helpless and wandering people, but as a process to educate and prepare the Israelites to put their total trust in God to supply their every need.

He was the food they ate. He was the clothing on their backs. He was the shoes on their feet. He was the covering over their heads. He was warmth for their bodies. In this experience, God was revealing Himself as Jehovah-Jireh, their all sufficient God. They were not, therefore, dependent upon other nations for their needs. They were dependent only upon God. They saw that they were not defenseless against the elements or at the mercy of the circumstances that surrounded them. Through God, they could conquer any circumstance.

But it was not enough for them to merely possess the land, to conquer through the miraculous. God's goal for this people was for them to have a relationship with Him. So, first, they must experience a restoration of the revelation of relationship, revelation of what it meant to be the chosen people of God.

God was revealing Himself through the miraculous, but the Law also worked toward this end. It had three dimensions: the civic dimension, the ceremonial dimension, and the spiritual or moral dimension. Each of these dimensions had a special lesson aimed to teach the people the holiness of God as they moved toward possession.

The civic dimension of the Law dealt with many aspects of the daily life of the people; for example, the dietary laws, the laws governing circumcision, and the laws governing communicable diseases. Many Bible scholars have failed to see more than a practical side to these laws. But I beg to differ with them. While there was a practical side to the laws given, relating to the health and welfare of the people, I am convinced that many of the laws had a much deeper purpose: that of reestablishing a unique national identity. God wanted the people of Israel to understand that there existed no other nation like theirs under the sun.

Circumcision obviously had some hygienic value, but it was not instituted for that purpose. It was instituted as a means of unique national identification.

The dietary laws obviously had some health aspects but that was not their primary purpose. Their primary purpose was to set Israel apart among the nations.

The laws governing Israel's social life— how they related to each other on a day-to-day basis — established norms of justice and honesty. But more than that, they dealt with identity. There was no other nation like Israel. The civic laws, therefore, taught Israel who they were because of Jehovah God.

The ceremonial laws governed the Tabernacle and how the people approached God, His glory, and His holiness. Through the ceremonial laws God gave His people a way of access into His glory. Before they could become a possessing people, before they could move into the Promised Land and possess their prophetic promise, they had to have access to the glory of God and access to His atonement. They had to learn to how approach Him and to be blessed in His presence.

The moral aspect of the Law dealt with issues of the heart. They taught Israel to be righteous before

God. The Ten Commandments, in particular, dealt with concepts of the righteousness of heart and spirit.

In the process of the wilderness experience, God also taught His people how to war. Soon after they had received the miracle of the water coming forth from the rock, Amalek was permitted to attack them; and those who lingered behind were slain. The animosity the Amalekites felt for the interlopers continued until the day Aaron and Hur held up the hands of Moses until the battle was finally won.

Through all of this, God was teaching His people that in order for them to be a conquering and victorious people, they would have to fight. Unlike other nations, however, they would not use normal military tactics. They would be spiritual warriors, conquering by obedience to His word.

The wilderness, therefore, was not intended to do God's people harm. It was for their good. It was a place of divine preparation. And each of us must go through his or her own personal "wilderness preparation" before we are able to cross over and become positionally ready to lay hold of our prophetic promises.

So, Moses' generation should have been ready; but they were not. When the first spies were sent into the land, the majority of them came back terrified saying, "We are nothing but grasshoppers compared to the giants who are in the land." It was only after this tragic display of lack of faith in Jehovah God that the judgments of the wilderness began to fall upon the children of Israel.

After all of God's miracles and provision (the manna, the fire, the cloud, the water out of the rock, the clothes and shoes that never wore out, etc.), after all that He had revealed of Himself and His nature (the civil, the ceremonial, and the moral law), after the way God had sustained and protected them for so many years, the hearts of the Israelite people had not substantially changed. They still were not convinced of who they were; and because of this, their generation was doomed to die in the wilderness. They could not possess their prophetic promise.

This was a generation poisoned by the slave mentality, by fear of the Egyptian lash, and by uncertainty about who they were and what their destiny in life was. When it came time to possess what God had prophetically promised them, the poison in their system destroyed their capacity to receive what He had prepared for them.

Thank God that the next generation embraced the revelation of identity and was able to pass over the Jordan. When the people of Jericho heard that the Israelites were coming, the Scriptures declare:

> *And they said unto Joshua, Truly the* LORD *hath delivered into our hands all the land; for even all the inhabitants of the country do faint because of us.* Joshua 2:24

The tide had clearly turned. Moses' generation was afraid of the inhabitants of Canaan, but now the in-

habitants of Canaan were afraid of this new generation, the possessors who replaced the fear-filled
generation that died in the wilderness.

This new generation knew who they were. They
were not poisoned by the remembrance of Egypt's
cruelties. They said, "We are able to take the land."
They had the spirit of Joshua and the spirit of Caleb,
not the spirit of Egypt. They were ready to march in
and begin to take what God had prepared for them.

If there is no spiritual revelation of who we are and
what our identity is in Christ, then, when we face the
giants who will certainly stand between` us and our
prophetic promise, we will crumble. We cannot face
adversity if we doubt who we are by the destiny of
our Lord Jesus Christ.

So, it wasn't that Moses' generation didn't know
about their prophetic promise. They had known
from the beginning. They were not delivered from
Egypt to wander in the wilderness. They were delivered from Egypt to possess the Promised Land. The
manna from heaven and the water from the rock
were miracles in their own right, but only temporary
blessings on the road to greater things. Yet, perhaps
out of fear of risking an invasion of the Promised
Land, many of them grew satisfied with the temporary and failed to press forward to the greater. Most
of them decided that if there were giants on the other
side, then they were better off where they were.

The known is always more comfortable than the
unknown; and many people miss God's best because
someone has sown seeds of fear in their hearts, tell-

ing them it is too hard to possess. But if God said we could possess it, then we can. Period! It doesn't matter how many giants are around. If God is with us, we can conquer any giant.

We are not being simplistic about this truth and recognize that there were other sins involved in Israel's failure to possess. Some of the children of Israel died in the wilderness because of murmuring and because of disrespect for God's leader, Moses. And any sin, if given full reign in your life, can rob you of God's best. I am convinced, however, that the thing that kept the people of Moses' generation on the far side of Jordan was their slave mentality, their failure mentality, and their maintenance mentality.

If you are satisfied to accept second best in your life, there isn't much God can do for you. He can show you the greater thing; but if you are content to remain behind in the lesser thing, He is powerless to force you to possess. If He did that, He would be taking away your free will, your personal freedom.

God loved Moses' generation and wanted something better for them than death in the desert, and He has something better for you. He does not intend to leave us in the desert. He is urging each of us not to be satisfied with a temporary blessing. The wilderness experience is only a step toward greater things, and He is urging each of us to press on to seek His best for our lives. Heed His call today and start *Possessing Your Prophetic Promise*.

Chapter 3

The Call to Possession

*Now after the death of Moses the servant of the
LORD it came to pass, that the LORD spake unto
Joshua the son of Nun, Moses' minister, saying,
Moses my servant is dead; now therefore arise,
go over this Jordan, thou, and all this people,
unto the land which I do give to them, even to
the children of Israel.*   Joshua 1:1-2

Today is a new day, a new hour, a new era; and
this is a new generation, different from any other that
has ever existed. We are all witnesses to the earth-
shaking changes that have rocked our world in

recent years. The changes in the physical realm have come because of changes in the spiritual realm. Many of the things that we are witnessing are not caused by Satan, as we might suppose, but by God Himself. He is orchestrating a worldwide change, as He sets the scene for a new move of His Spirit.

We have only to read the newspaper or to watch the evening news to know that we are in the last days of time. Here in America, there is an unprecedented rise in violent crime, political corruption, and sexual perversion. The American people are being abused as never before: child abuse, wife abuse, and sexual harassment in the workplace. And these problems do not stem from overpopulation, illegal immigration, or lack of education. Instead, the great tragedy of evil influences over our society is a result of the Church's failure to rise up and be what God has called it to be. God has not called you and me to be members of a Christian country club. We are called to change lives. We are called to provide a place of refuge for the hurting. We are called to present an answer to the world to the all-pervasive problems people face every day.

Satan is rearing his ugly head with more boldness than ever before; and we cannot fight him successfully with the CIA, the FBI, or the local police department. The only weapon we have against the enemy is the power of the Holy Ghost. Words will not do the job. It was true in the Apostle Paul's day, as well:

And my speech and my preaching was not with enticing words of man's wisdom, but in demonstration of the Spirit and of power:

> 1 Corinthians 2:4

The answer lies not in the intervention of a particular denomination or a particular individual. The Body of Christ as a whole, men and women of every church who love the Lord and are born of His Spirit, must return to God's Word and determine to *live* by the principles taught there. When we do that, we will see that we *can* make a difference in our world.

We have recently been blessed by the greatest period of expository teaching of the Word of God that any generation has ever experienced. We now have more resources available to us than ever before: cassette tapes, videos, books, and television and radio programs. Some of the best Bible teachers that have ever stood in the pulpit are feeding our spirits these days. Why? God is sowing in our hearts to prepare us for what lies ahead. It is time to possess our prophetic promises.

Now is not the time to be sitting in the spiritual classroom for long periods of time. It is time to graduate and move on to putting to practical use the knowledge and wisdom we have gained. God is saying to us, "It is time to get out of medical school and into the operating room, out of the drawing room and onto the construction site. I want you to quit talking and start acting!"

Too many Christians have become professional religious students. They would be content to stay in training for the rest of their lives. But God needs some surgeons. He needs some people who won't faint when Satan's victims are wheeled into the emergency room of the Spirit. He needs people who know how to use the tools He has put in their hands. Most of us still panic when the emergency comes and wonder, *What page do I turn to?* Take those spiritual weapons down from the shelf and let the use of them become a natural and spontaneous part of your everyday life.

Like those who died on the other side of the Jordan, too many Christians are leading a "maintenance walk." They're holding on to yesterday's blessings and are afraid to reach out for anything new. They have a maintenance mentality. They live constantly within a certain comfort zone and then wonder why Christianity is no longer exciting to them. The truth is that those people miss the most exciting things that God has for them. Right now, God has some things prepared for this generation that are more exciting than we have ever dreamed. We are on the brink of revival. God has something fresh to say to this Church, and it is time for us to rise up and receive it. We must cast off our fear of new things and boldly open ourselves to the will of God. Paul said:

> *Brethren, I count not myself to have apprehended: but this one thing I do, forgetting those things which are behind, and reaching forth*

*unto those things which are before, I press to-
ward the mark for the prize of the high calling of
God in Christ Jesus.* Philippians 3:13-14

This is a new hour in God. The sun is rising on a
new and exciting adventure, and the generation of
maintenance is coming to an end. It is time to move
on. Moses represented the generation that died in the
wilderness. So, God said to Joshua, *"Moses, my servant, is dead."* It was time to move on, time to launch
forth, time to possess. What Moses had was good,
but today God is leading us into a fuller understanding of His goodness. It is time to possess.

During recent years, we have learned a lot about
maintaining our Christian walk. We've been taught
how to maintain our blessing, how to maintain har-
mony in our homes, and how to maintain a prayer
life. And we will not despise any of that. It is all
important. Without this knowledge, acquired
through years of wandering in the wilderness, we
would be destroyed in this new spiritual hour.

What we will do is use the knowledge we have
gained as a building block to take us to higher places
with God. When the medical student leaves the classroom, he doesn't leave behind the knowledge he has
gained. Instead, he takes that knowledge with him
and puts it into action in the medical field.

God told Joshua that it was now time to move on,
that he was to take this opportunity to arise and cross
over the Jordan with all the people. What awaited

them? The Promised Land. It was still there for the taking, still waiting for a bold generation to possess it.

The fact that Moses had died did not mean that the Israelites were to abandon the truths that he had taught them. Crossing the Jordan was not a step backward, but a step forward. It did not mean giving up the old. It meant moving into something new and better.

There comes a point in our lives when we must do more than simply survive; we must know more than just enough to get by in life; and we must do more with the knowledge we have gained than just maintain our spiritual lives. I know people today who have just exactly what they had forty years ago. They have nothing more to eat, nothing more to wear, and nothing more to walk in (spiritually speaking).

That is a shame because the time has come for us to rise up in God and declare:

There is more for my family.
There is more for my church.
There is more for my city.
There is more for my country.
I want all that God says I can have.
I will possess my prophetic promise.

We must rise up as warriors and say, "Devil, enough is enough. You have occupied my Promised Land for too long, and now I'm going to chase you out and possess what is rightfully mine."

I love to sing from Psalms 68:

> *Let God arise, let his enemies be scattered.*
> Psalms 68:1

What a powerful song! But, it must become more than just a song to us; and in order for God to arise, you and I must also arise. Why? Because Christ is in us:

> *To whom God would make known what is the riches of the glory of this mystery among the Gentiles; which is Christ in you, the hope of glory:* Colossians 1:27

> *I am crucified with Christ: nevertheless I live; yet not I, but Christ liveth in me.*
> Galatians 2:20

If God does not arise, then we will not see our enemies scattered; and if God is to arise, we must also arise. As we arise, He will arise in us and through us.

If we do not arise, then the enemy will continue to feast on the milk and honey of our Promised Land; he will continue to confiscate our health and prosperity and our peace and joy; he will continue to cause the breakup of relationships between family and friends, parent and child, and husband and wife.

If we do not arise and take the land, we are destined to see more bigotry, prejudice, and hatred than ever before. We will continue to stand helplessly by as drug use, sexual perversion, and gang violence escalate. These evils will not be resolved by some special task force. They will be stopped only when God's people take authority over and break the power of the evil spirits that are driving people.

There is more to Christianity than sitting in an easy chair flipping the channels on your television set. We are in a war. And if the Church does not rise up and get God's vision for our lives, for our families, for our cities, for our nations, and for our world, we will never be able to stop the evil that is destroying us.

Comfort is not a bad thing — in itself. But don't get so comfortable that you are not ready to move on. Don't get so comfortable that you lose sight of what is up ahead. Don't get so comfortable that you lose the vision of the Promised Land. Don't get so comfortable that you forget your prophetic promise.

Some people seek comforts to fill a void in their lives. As believers, we are instructed to be *"filled with the Spirit"* instead (Ephesians 5:18). This means more than just speaking in tongues. It means being so full of God that other things in your life dim in importance. Get so full of the Spirit that there is no room for religious philosophies, for prejudices, for drugs, or for depression. Move into the *"liberty"* of the Holy Spirit:

> *Now the Lord is that Spirit: and where the Spirit of the Lord is, there is liberty.*
> 2 Corinthians 3:17

If you want to remain a slave, you will remain a slave. If you want to stay on second base, you will stay on second base. If you want to live a life of spiritual maintenance, you will do so. But I say to you today, it is time to rise up and scatter the enemy from the land. It is time to possess what is rightfully ours, that which God has promised to us prophetically.

God cannot force you to do it, just as He could not force Moses' generation to cross the Jordan. He wanted them to do it and let them know that they could do it. But they chose not to. In the end, what you possess is a matter of your own choice. Don't blame God for your predicament. His will for your life is perfect. He has wonderful things just waiting for you. The choice is yours. Will you be satisfied to maintain the status quo? Or will you be one of those who march in to take the land?

God didn't send Joshua into the Promised Land alone. He told him to take *"all this people"* with him. That is very important for those of us who are chosen to lead. I have known too many great men of God who received the revelation of an inheritance from God and were transformed from death into life, from sickness into health, and from poverty into prosperity. When they tried to share this revelation with God's people, however, they met with apathy and, in the end, went on into the promised land alone. This is clearly not God's plan. He wants us to go in together, as a mighty band of believers.

Joshua and Caleb were among the first who tried to convince the children of Israel that they were capable of defeating their enemies and possessing the land. Because of that, they were permitted to lead the people across safely to the other side. But they did not go alone. The Promised Land is not just for dynamic leaders. It is for all of God's people. He is not pleased when a few enter, leaving the majority behind in the wilderness.

God needs more than a few *"with healing in their hands."* He needs more than a few to stand with prophetic utterance. He needs more than a few who have received a revelation of health, prosperity, faith, prayer, and the blessings of God. He is calling more than one and more than a few. His call is for all of His people — an entire generation of believers — to arise and obey the call to possession.

Chapter 4

The Promise of Possession

Every place that the sole of your foot shall tread upon, that have I given unto you, as I said unto Moses. From the wilderness and this Lebanon even unto the great river, the river Euphrates, all the land of the Hittites, and unto the great sea toward the going down of the sun, shall be your coast. There shall not any man be able to stand before thee all the days of thy life: as I was with Moses, so I will be with thee: I will not fail thee, nor forsake thee. Be strong and of a good courage: for unto this people shalt thou divide for an inheritance the land, which I sware unto their fathers to give them. Joshua 1:3-6

God has given us a promise of possession, and we must understand it and accept it. We make two major mistakes in this regard: (1) we try to figure out what we want in life, and (2) we are too easily satisfied with something less than God's best.

You don't know what is best for your life. Your understanding is so far inferior to God's that it is utterly foolish for you to decide what you want in life and work toward that goal. God's ways are best. Don't settle for anything less. Understand what God has prepared for you; quit trying to figure out what to prepare for yourself, and be satisfied with what GOD has prepared for you.

God didn't tell Joshua and the Israelites to take over the whole world. He set clearly defined boundaries and showed them what land was theirs to possess. One of the major downfalls of churches and ministries today is that they are going after things that they want, not things that God has designated for them.

When you take yourself out from under the covering of God's provision and protection, you either succeed on your own talent or you fail; and most people fail. Why waste your energy and talents fighting for something that God has not destined you to have? Do you doubt His goodness? Do you think you know better than God? When you insist on doing your own will, you are no longer in a position to receive His help. You are on your own.

When we discover what God wants us to do — as individuals, as families, as a Church, or as a ministry — we can boldly cross over Jordan and run any giant right out of the land. But be sure you stay within the borders of your land.

And don't worry! God has plenty of blessings prepared for you:

> *Only be thou strong and very courageous, that thou mayest observe to do according to all the law, which Moses my servant commanded thee: turn not from it to the right hand or to the left, that thou mayest prosper whithersoever thou goest. This book of the law shall not depart out of thy mouth; but thou shalt meditate therein day and night, that thou mayest observe to do according to all that is written therein: for then thou shalt make thy way prosperous, and then thou shalt have good success.* Joshua 1:7-8

To successfully drive out the enemy and occupy our Promised Land, we must be careful to live according to the Word of God. Too many people try to bring their sins into the church and get God's approval on their lifestyle. They want God's blessings, but they also want to continue some of their former habits. They are part of a generation of compromisers, and that was the sin that destroyed Samson. He thought he could lie in bed with a harlot one moment and the next moment shake himself and still have the same power with God he had before. For a while, it seemed to work; but his end was sad.

Some people think they can live in rebellion six days a week and come to church on Sunday to receive God's blessing. They have a lot to learn. Compromise does not bring anointing; it does not break the yokes of bondage; it will not heal the sick; it cannot reunite husbands and wives; it will never deliver young people from drugs. We must have a touch from God in order to cause our enemies to flee, and the only way to obtain the touch of God upon your life is to clean up your act and keep it clean. And in order to maintain a godly lifestyle, we must return to the principles of fasting, praying, and seeking God's righteousness.

Some people think they can enter the Promised Land and live among the heathen there. But God told the children of Israel to drive out the heathen before them. **Full possession requires that we make no compromise with the enemy.** He must be driven out if we are to possess all that God has promised us prophetically.

When David became king over Israel, He was determined to rid the land of the evil influence of the heathen. He had much success, and under his reign Israel made great gains. But at one point, David himself fell into sin:

> *And it came to pass, after the year was expired, at the time when kings go forth to battle, that David sent Joab, and his servants with him, and all Israel; and they destroyed the children of*

> Ammon, and besieged Rabbah. But David tar-
> ried still at Jerusalem. And it came to pass in an
> eveningtide, that David arose from off his bed,
> and walked upon the roof of the king's house:
> and from the roof he saw a woman washing her-
> self; and the woman was very beautiful to look
> upon. And David sent and inquired after the
> woman. And one said, Is not this Bathsheba, the
> daughter of Eliam, the wife of Uriah the Hittite?
> And David sent messengers, and took her; and
> she came in unto him, and he lay with her; for
> she was purified from her uncleanness: and she
> returned unto her house.   2 Samuel 11:1-4

It was time for war, not for relaxing. It was time to drive out enemy kings, not to get comfortable and give the flesh a break. Surely, as king, David had the right to stay home in relative safety. Sure, David had a lot of business to take care of in Jerusalem. And, sure, Joab was a capable military leader. But David was a soldier and should have been on the battle-field. We need all the soldiers we can get, and we all need to stay on the front lines of battle and give no place to the flesh. Don't get too tired to pray. Don't get too tired to do battle with the enemy of your soul. Press on to possession.

The results of David's unwise decision to pander to the flesh was his adultery with Bathsheba and his complicity in the murder of her husband, Uriah. In one moment of letting down his guard, David brought more sorrow and pain upon his own life, his household, and his nation than anything his enemies could have devised.

Let us learn from David's example. We are *"kings and priests unto God"*:

> *And hath made us kings and priests unto God and his Father; to him be glory and dominion for ever and ever. Amen.*   Revelation 1:6

Let us be faithful kings, always ready for battle, always faithful on the front lines. Let us go forth boldly into battle. We have a promise of possession.

David's failure was in slipping back into the maintenance mentality. Much had been accomplished, so he was satisfied to stay home this time. But we will not win this battle in our easy chairs. It is time to go forth and face the enemy.

Many people refuse to fight. They would rather die in the wilderness. They would rather be at peace with the little they now have than to press on into more complete victory. They want to stay on the other side of Jordan, and they will die in the wilderness.

Some are afraid of the giants. They believe the reports of the doubting spies:

> *And there we saw the giants, the sons of Anak, which come of the giants: and we were in our own sight as grasshoppers, and so we were in their sight.*   Numbers 13:33

When your self-perception is that you are an insect under the foot of a giant, you are not ready to fight. And that is a major problem in the church today. We have looked at the giants of the political system, the giants of the drug epidemic, the giants of the gang violence, the giants of recession, the giants of bigotry and hatred; and we have felt that we are not up to the battle, that this thing is too big for us.

Thank God that two of the spies came back with a different story:

> *And Caleb stilled the people before Moses, and said, Let us go up at once, and possess it; for we are well able to overcome it.*   Numbers 13:30

"We are well able." We can do this thing. Stop looking at the giants. We have a promise of possession. God said we could have it; and if God said it, I believe it. The difference in Joshua's and Caleb's report was that it was a report of faith. They didn't deny that the giants existed. They didn't deny that the battle would be fierce. But they said, *"We are well able."* That's why they didn't die on the other side of the Jordan with the rest of that crowd.

They were ready to face giants in order to get what was theirs. Caleb had seen all the giants on his mountain. Yet, he said, *"Give me this mountain"*:

> *Now therefore give me this mountain, whereof the* LORD *spake in that day; for thou heardest in*

that day how the Anakims were there, and that
the cities were great and fenced: if so be the LORD
will be with me, then I shall be able to drive them
out, as the LORD *said.*   Joshua 14:12

Faith knows that the Lord is with us and that *"I*
shall be able to drive them out." Caleb wasn't too tired
to face his mountain full of giants. He had a prophetic promise of possession: *"as the* LORD *said."*

Don't be afraid to reach out for something new.
Too many people are afraid to even try. They are so
afraid of failure. They are so afraid to be laughed at.
They are so afraid to be misunderstood. They consider dying on the other side of Jordan to be better
than trying something new.

Some people would rather stay sick; then they
avoid the disappointment of not getting healed if
they are prayed for. They would rather be sick than
disappointed; they would rather be sick than
misunderstood; they would rather be sick than
laughed at. What a sad state! They would rather hold
on to the little they have than risk facing the giants to
gain the very best.

Joshua sent his own spies:

And they said unto Joshua, Truly the LORD *hath*
delivered into our hands all the land; for even all
the inhabitants of the country do faint because of
us.   Joshua 2:24

Notice, they said nothing about giants. Those *"gi-*
ants" were scared to death because they had heard

that God's people were coming after them. If you could just get this truth down in your spirit, you could shake the world for God.

The evil report of the first spies had kept a whole generation from possessing. Now, the giants were still there. The military capabilities of Israel had not improved significantly. So, what was the difference? It was the difference between faith and fear, between vision and the comfort zone, between maintaining and conquering. This new generation had a different attitude, a different mentality. This new generation had experienced the *"renewing"* of their minds:

> *And be not conformed to this world: but be ye transformed by the renewing of your mind.*
> Romans 12:2

They stopped believing they were grasshoppers and began believing what God said. And, when they did, their attitudes completely changed. They had "crossing-over" attitudes. They were no longer satisfied just to maintain the status quo. Thank God for the discontentment He sometimes places in your spirit. It is not a bad thing. It is a holy vision, a holy drive, to move you out of your apathy and into victory.

God told Elijah to stay by the brook Cherith and that He would sustain him there:

> *Get thee hence, and turn thee eastward, and hide thyself by the brook Cherith, that is before*

> *Jordan. And it shall be, that thou shalt drink of*
> *the brook; and I have commanded the ravens to*
> *feed thee there. So he went and did according*
> *unto the word of the* LORD: *for he went and*
> *dwelt by the brook Cherith, that is before Jordan.*
>   1 Kings 17:3-5

What a wonderful way to live! God was providing miraculously for Elijah's every need. But one day God told him to leave that place and go to Zarephath. I can imagine that Elijah was very reluctant. I can hear him talking to God: "Oh no, God. Here I have got food and water; and You've been meeting all my other needs here, as well. Besides, the people of Zarephath hate me."

Apparently Elijah was hesitant to leave such a wonderful place, so God had to allow the brook to dry up so that He could get the prophet's attention. When the ravens came to get Elijah's food, God said to them, "Don't take Elijah any more food. Go do what ravens do. I'll take care of Elijah myself now."

When Elijah began to seriously wonder what was happening in his life, God spoke to him:

> *Arise, get thee to Zarephath, which belongeth to*
> *Zidon, and dwell there: behold, I have com-*
> *manded a widow woman there to sustain thee.*
>   1 Kings 17:9

God hadn't forgotten His servant; He just had something new for him. He had not forsaken Elijah; He was just leading him on to greater things.

When calamities come our way, the immediate reaction of many of us is to murmur. Then when some time has passed and we finally understand what God has been doing in our lives, we thank Him for those "calamities." Many of the troublesome feelings, the discontented feelings, the unsatisfied feelings we all have are from God, and their purpose is to lead us on to greater things. If you are suddenly tired of eating manna, perhaps you are ready for some milk and honey.

It is no longer enough just to be part of the family of God. It is no longer enough just to believe in His miracles. It is no longer enough just to understand His ways. It is time to possess all that He has promised us.

The fearful need not apply to God's army in these days. When God chose Gideon to deliver his people from the Midianites, one of the first things He did was to separate the fearful from the ranks of the volunteers and send them on their way home. God can't use the fearful and unbelieving:

> *And the* LORD *said unto Gideon, The people that are with thee are too many for me to give the Midianites into their hands, lest Israel vaunt themselves against me, saying, Mine own hand hath saved me. Now therefore go to, proclaim in the ears of the people, saying, Whosoever is fearful and afraid, let him return and depart early from mount Gilead. And there returned of the*

> *people twenty and two thousand; and there re-*
> *mained ten thousand.*   Judges 7:2-3

It seems difficult to believe that we have "too many" soldiers. We think that we need more. But God said there were "too many." He put them to a further test: those who laid down their weapons because they saw the watering hole as a playground instead of a place of refreshing and preparation were to be sent home. When Gideon had obeyed, there remained only 300 of the original 32,000. Those faithful 300 warriors didn't lay down their weapons for a moment, even to drink. They drank with a sword in one hand and didn't lower their eyes. They were not about to give the enemy an advantage over them — even for a moment. That's the type of warrior God is seeking in these days.

We need to grow up and get serious with God. We need to pray and fast, sanctify ourselves, and prepare for serious battle. Let us say, "We are determined to possess everything that God has promised us. Nothing will deter us. Every enemy will faint because of us. Let us arise and cross over."

"Renewing" our minds by the Spirit of God prepares us for possession. We no longer have the old mind set. We know that we need no longer wait, and we are afraid of nothing. The grasshopper mentality has disappeared. And it is time to possess.

We refuse to sit back while the devil confiscates everything that is rightfully ours. We will no longer stand idly by while he torments our loved ones. We are determined to take possession of our prophetic promise. We know we are God's warriors, capable of harvesting souls, healing the sick, breaking bondages, reconciling homes, delivering the oppressed, loosing the chains of poverty, and setting people free by the power of the Holy Spirit.

We are eager to climb that mountain full of giants because we know that God will surely give us the victory. We have the promise of possession.

Chapter 5

Crossing Over Into Possession

And Joshua rose early in the morning; and they removed from Shittim, and came to Jordan, he and all the children of Israel, and lodged there before they passed over. And it came to pass after three days, that the officers went through the host; And they commanded the people, saying, When ye see the ark of the covenant of the LORD *your God, and the priests the Levites bearing it, then ye shall remove from your place, and go after it.*   Joshua 3:1-3

If Joshua were a modern-day saint, that passage might have begun something like this:

And Joshua rose up early in the morning, put on his robe and had several cups of coffee while watching "Good Morning America."

Thank God it doesn't say that. Joshua rose early in the morning to commune with God in preparation for crossing into the Promised Land to possess his prophetic promises; and if we want to possess our promises in God, we will have to do the same. God has given many of us a divine understanding that we are getting ready to experience a greater move of the Spirit. Those who are rising early to prepare themselves for it are gathering on the banks of the Jordan, ready to cross over into their Promised Land.

Before the children of Israel could possess the Promised Land, they had to *"remove from [their] places."* It is impossible to move into the new if you are unwilling to leave the old. If you are satisfied in the place you are now, you can never make further progress. *"Remove from your places."*

We have no trouble finding many saints of God. They are in the same place they have been for as long as we can remember. They haven't moved an inch. They can't seem to recognize that it is time to take a new direction, time to act on God's promises, time to cross over into possession.

When the Ark moved, the children of Israel knew it was time for them to move. The Ark of the Covenant was a symbol of God's presence to the wilderness believers. God's glory dwelled there. It was there that He accepted their sacrifices. And it was there that He communed with the priests in the Tabernacle. Now God told them to follow the Ark. When the Ark moved, they were to move; and when the Ark stopped, they were to stop. What simple instruction: follow the glory of the Lord.

Shake yourself and move on with the glory of God. The Ark is moving. Get loosed from the place of mere survival and move on into the place of abundance. The Ark is moving.

Don't worry about your safety and the safety of your family and friends. The place of safety is the place where the glory of God is. You can't lose when you move with the glory. Nothing could be safer.

David chose to stay home and be safe, and we saw what happened to him. Safety is relative. You are safe in the will of God for your life. You are safe when you are following His leading, wherever it may take you.

When we make a "logical decision" based on human wisdom and we disregard the wisdom of God, we are in trouble. When man's logical reasoning opposes God's will, no matter how brilliant that reasoning may seem, it will always result in death. True safety is found only in the perfect will of God.

By staying home, David took himself out from under God's covering and glory. As a result, he made a series of wrong decisions that brought death and cursing to his household. What David thought was a place of safety was really a place of destruction. Be careful. Make your decisions based on God's Word and His will, and not on your own desires and your feelings of what represents safety for you. God knows better than you do. Follow the Ark:

> *Yet there shall be a space between you and it, about two thousand cubits by measure: come not near unto it, that ye may know the way by which ye must go: for ye have not passed this way heretofore.*   Joshua 3:4

We can no longer be satisfied to do the same things over and over. God is leading us into new things. He is taking us deeper and higher. He has ordained things for us that we have not yet moved into. He has promised us territory that we have not yet possessed. And we don't know the way. *"Ye have not passed this way heretofore."* Follow the Ark:

> *And Joshua said unto the people, Sanctify yourselves: for to morrow the* LORD *will do wonders among you.*   Joshua 3:5

For every new thing God has promised us, there is a required preparation on our part. The reason most of us rarely see tomorrows full of the wonders of the Lord is that we fail to prepare today for what tomorrow holds. We fail to see God's glory tomorrow because we fail to *sanctify* ourselves today.

That word *"sanctify"* means *"to make holy"* or *"to set apart for divine use."* Holiness is not just a matter of outward appearance. It is more than changing the type of clothing you wear. It is more than your hair style. Holiness begins in the heart and works its way out. So when Joshua told the children of Israel to *sanctify* themselves, he meant for them to deal with the spiritual condition of their hearts. If your heart is not right before God, you will never move into possession. *Sanctify yourselves:*

> *And Joshua spake unto the priests, saying, Take up the ark of the covenant, and pass over before the people. And they took up the ark of the covenant, and went before the people. And the* LORD *said unto Joshua, This day will I begin to magnify thee in the sight of all Israel, that they may know that, as I was with Moses, so I will be with thee.* Joshua 3:6-7

Next, God moved to secure Joshua's position of authority with the people. He was *"magnify[ing]"* Joshua in the sight of the people because Joshua was a type of Christ. The Hebrew word *"Joshua"* means the same as the Greek word *"Jesus," "salvation"* or *"savior."* Joshua was magnified, or exalted, at the Jordan River, just as Jesus would be centuries later:

> *And Jesus, when he was baptized, went up straightway out of the water: and, lo, the heavens were opened unto him, and he saw the Spirit of God descending like a dove, and lighting upon him: And lo a voice from heaven, saying, This is my beloved Son, in whom I am well pleased.* Matthew 3:16-17

Joshua was more than just the head of Israel's government. He was a man of God. He stood with the Ark of God's glory while the children of Israel crossed over into their Promised Land. This was a prophetic foretelling that Jesus Christ would be the power and the glory of God, the fullness of the Godhead, and would translate men from death into life, from the wilderness of sin into God's Promised Land. Praise God!

> *And thou shalt command the priests that bear the ark of the covenant, saying, When ye are come to the brink of the water of Jordan, ye shall stand still in Jordan.*   Joshua 3:8

Why did the priests have to stand still in the Jordan? They stood still because they were waiting for a miracle from God. There are many things you *can* do to move toward possession, but there are also many things you *can't* do. And you will never possess your prophetic promises without the miracles of God to aide you.

You *can* sanctify yourself. You *can* break loose from the place you have been living until now and determine to move forward to other things. You *can* decide to follow God's glory and to respect His leadership. But the only way you will ever cross over into the Promised Land is through a miracle from God. I've never yet met a person who could cause rivers to part. Parting the Jordan required a supernatural touch from God. And without that supernatural touch on your life, you will make little progress toward the realization of your dream.

We will never move beyond miracles. NEVER! If we are to take a city, if we are to shake a nation, if we are to bring about change in people's lives, then we need miracles. We simply can't do it alone.

Many of us have memorized formulas that we think can accomplish anything at all. But none of our formulas can ever part rivers. Only God can part rivers. It is time to take our faith out of the formulas and put it in God. He alone can part the waters.

For some people the parting of the waters only brings fear because it makes them vulnerable to the giants on the other side. Fear blinds them to the opened river before them. All they can see and think about are the giants. Those people will never see Jordan opened. If God can part the waters of the Jordan, He can give you victory over the giants on the other side. If God can allow you to *"walk across on dry ground,"* He can take care of any giant that you may face as a result.

Some people will never cross over until God kills all the giants on the other side. Well, they will never cross over because God is opening the waters so that we can go forth and drive out the giants. The giants will never disappear as long as you stay on the other side in relative safety and ease. Cross over with faith that God will drive out the giants before you:

> *And Joshua said, Hereby ye shall know that the living God is among you, and that he will*

> *without fail drive out from before you the Ca-*
> *naanites, and the Hittites, and the Hivites, and*
> *the Perizzites, and the Girgashites, and the*
> *Amorites, and the Jebusites. Behold, the ark of*
> *the covenant of the* LORD *of all the earth passeth*
> *over before you into Jordan.*
>
> Joshua 3:10-11

"Without fail." You will not take the land without a fight, but don't let that discourage you. God will fight for you. He will go before you to destroy your enemies. If you worry about enemies, you will never achieve what God wants you to achieve. If you worry about enemies, you will never be what God wants you to be. If you worry about enemies, you will never go where God wants you to go. Let God take care of the enemies. He will do it *"without fail."*

The devil wants you to stay in the wilderness. He doesn't mind that God is sustaining you there with manna. He doesn't mind hearing you say that your clothes don't wear out and that you are enjoying the protection of the cloud and the pillar of fire. He's happy because you're not taking the Promised Land away from him. HE IS ENJOYING YOUR MILK AND HONEY.

The maintenance mentality presents no threat to Satan's kingdom. What he fears are the conquerors, those who cross over and possess. It is only when you cross over that you become a threat to his dominion.

The devil wants to stop prayer warriors from praying, evangelists from evangelizing, exhorters from exhorting, teachers from teaching, and pastors from pastoring. Why? If he can keep them merely existing on the other side of Jordan, his kingdom is safe.

I don't know about you, but I am determined to cross over into those fertile valleys of the Promised Land. I want to enjoy their prosperity and to share it with others — whatever the cost. And there *are* many battles ahead. You can be sure of that. But we have nothing to fear. With God on our side, we are giant killers. When we cross over, God has the opportunity to prove that He is with us by giving us the victory.

Sidestepping battles doesn't prove anything. How does that glorify God? We need to get our thinking straightened out. The greater the battle, the greater the victory. Avoiding conflict proves nothing at all.

When you are doing what God has called you to do, going where God has called you to go, and saying what God has called you to say, you *will* face opposition but you will also prosper and walk in God's blessing. If you are following God's direction, you will be safer on the forefront of the battle than you would be waiting behind the front lines in the wilderness. When you go where God is leading, even if they've heated up the furnace seven times hotter than usual (see Daniel 3:19), you will find that God has gotten there before you and will be with you in the fire to deliver you. There is more safety on God's battle front than in the security you have created for yourself.

Be willing to fight for your blessing and not just take what the devil hands you in life. This is not a game. Don't take it lightly. We are fighting a war for our land, our youth, our loved ones, our homes, our blessings, our Promised Land.

The principles that guided Israel to the crossing of the Jordan are valid for us in the closing years of the twentieth century. We must:

1. Lose the grasshopper mentality by experiencing the renewing of our minds.

2. Sanctify ourselves, purify our hearts, so that God can show us His wonders.

3. Be willing to leave our previous place of security and follow the glory of God.

4. Wait for God to move on our behalf and believe Him for a miracle.

If we follow these steps, we cannot fail. God will drive out our enemies before us and give us possession of our Promised Land. Cross over now into possession.

Chapter 6

Preparation for Possession

*And it came to pass, when all the people were
clean passed over Jordan, that the* LORD *spake
unto Joshua, saying, Take you twelve men out of
the people, out of every tribe a man,*
*And Joshua said unto them, Pass over before the
ark of the* LORD *your God into the midst of Jordan, and take ye up every man of you a stone
upon his shoulder, according unto the number of
the tribes of the children of Israel: That this may
be a sign among you, that when your children
ask their fathers in time to come, saying, What
mean ye by these stones? Then ye shall answer*

them, That the waters of Jordan were cut off before the ark of the covenant of the LORD; when it
passed over Jordan, the waters of Jordan were
cut off: and these stones shall be for a memorial
unto the children of Israel for ever.

Joshua 4:1-2 & 5-7

Some people think they are ready to conquer their
Promised Land. After all, they are full of the Word of
God and have learned to use the weapons of spiritual
warfare. They're eager for a fight. "Just point me in
the direction of battle," they seem to be saying.

I would offer a word of caution. This is not a game.
This is serious warfare, and there are certain prepa-
rations we all need to make to ensure victory in
battle. As we see by Israel's example, crossing over is
one thing, but possessing is quite another. They had
to prepare for possession.

The first thing the children of Israel did after crossing over the Jordan was to build a memorial, a
permanent reminder of the miracles of God. It was
an act of thanksgiving to God and of recognition that
without Him they were nothing. That is an important
first step. Don't get too cocky when you cross over
successfully. You didn't do it on your own, nor could
you have done it. Stay humble, and remain thankful
to God.

When success comes, we are so quick to forget
Who the Author of that success really was. But un-
grateful people will never possess. When Israel
forgot the goodness of God and became lifted up

with self-importance, God had His way of humbling her:

> *Because thou servedst not the* LORD *thy God*
> *with joyfulness, and with gladness of heart, for*
> *the abundance of all things; Therefore shalt thou*
> *serve thine enemies which the* LORD *shall send*
> *against thee, in hunger, and in thirst, and in*
> *nakedness, and in want of all things: and he*
> *shall put a yoke of iron upon thy neck, until he*
> *have destroyed thee.*
>
> Deuteronomy 28:47-48

We must never forget how deep in the pit we were before God saved us. That is one of the reasons for the regular celebration of communion:

> *This is my body which is given for you: this do*
> *in remembrance of me.* Luke 22:19

The communion table is for us what that memorial was for the children of Israel. It is a time of remembering and of giving thanks for what God has done for us.

Such a memorial is a fortress against pride; for when we remember where we came from, pride, that most destructive of human tendencies, cannot overtake us:

> *Pride goeth before destruction, and an haughty*
> *spirit before a fall.* Proverbs 16:18

Thankful people have no room for pride. Thankful people dwell on the greatness of God, never on the greatness of self. Thankful people remember, and thankful people are continually humbled by their memories.

Monuments have always had great significance for the people of any nation. We, as Americans, are moved when we see the Statue of Liberty in New York Harbor. It is a constant reminder to us that America was established as a haven for the world's poor and hurting, *"the huddled masses,"* and that each of us is descended from someone who first found refuge here. The Statue of Liberty is, thus, a symbol of hope and freedom.

The memorial erected by Joshua and the children of Israel that day at Jordan was just as significant. It would be a constant reminder to generations to come that their ancestors were slaves in Egypt and pilgrims in the wilderness and that through the mercy and power of God a new generation had crossed over and taken possession of a bountiful land — for the benefit of all succeeding generations.

The memorial would serve as an inspiration during the battles that would come, a reminder that the first step of possession had been accomplished and that further steps were possible — if Israel kept on the prescribed course. In time to come, the people would think to themselves: *Now, wait a minute. If God could part the waters before us so that we walked across on dry ground, then why can't He bring me through this present situation?*

Many generations of Israelites were destined to draw faith from that memorial, a constant reminder to their spirits of the miracles God had already done and a challenge to completely possess everything He had promised them.

Many Christians are very thankful when everything is going well. When a battle comes their way, however, they not only quit thanking God, they actually become despondent and begin to murmur and complain. We are so quick to start moaning and groaning, as if we expected to move God's hand by our pitifulness. But God doesn't inhabit our pitifulness. He inhabits our praises (see Psalms 22:3).

When you're in the midst of a battle, you must remember the victories of the past and begin thanking God for His salvation in the present. Memorials serve that purpose. They remind us of His goodness and faithfulness to us in the past. And, when we remember what God has done for us in the past, faith rises up in our hearts for the present situation:

> *And it came to pass, when all the kings of the Amorites, which were on the side of Jordan westward, and all the kings of the Canaanites, which were by the sea, heard that the* LORD *had dried up the waters of Jordan from before the children of Israel, until we were passed over, that their heart melted, neither was there spirit in them any more, because of the children of Israel. At that time the* LORD *said unto Joshua, Make thee*

sharp knives, and circumcise again the children of Israel the second time.

And it came to pass, when they had done circumcising all the people, that they abode in their places in the camp, till they were whole.

Joshua 5:1-2 & 8

The second thing Joshua did after crossing the Jordan River was to circumcise all the men of Israel. Circumcision is a cutting away of the flesh of the foreskin. In the New Testament, however, circumcision is of the heart and represents a cutting away of the fleshly nature of a man or woman:

In whom also ye are circumcised with the circumcision made without hands, in putting off the body of the sins of the flesh by the circumcision of Christ: Colossians 2:11

For he is not a Jew, which is one outwardly; neither is that circumcision, which is outward in the flesh: But he is a Jew, which is one inwardly; and circumcision is that of the heart, in the spirit, and not in the letter; whose praise is not of men, but of God. Romans 2:28-29

For we are the circumcision, which worship God in the spirit, and rejoice in Christ Jesus, and have no confidence in the flesh.

Philippians 3:3

What does it mean to circumcise your flesh nature? The things we think of immediately that need to be cut away are drunkenness and drug addiction, smoking, cursing, adultery and fornication, stealing, lying, and cheating your boss. These are all things that must be cut away. But there is more to it than that. These are only symptoms of the fleshly nature, and removing the symptoms is not enough.

Your flesh yearns to dominate your spirit and to rule over it. If you let it happen, your flesh will dictate how far you can go with God, how much you can receive from God, and even how much you can serve God. The flesh delights in filling our lives with clutter that hinders us and keeps us from being what God has destined us to be.

The flesh insists:

> *I'm too tired to serve God.*
> *I'm too busy to serve God.*
> *I'm afraid to make changes because it may disrupt my comfort zone.*

I'd like to meet the man who is actually better off by sleeping an extra hour in the morning rather than rising and spending that time in prayer, as the Spirit urges us to do. If flesh can trick you in these small ways, Satan can keep you from God's very best.

Far too many Christians today think that they can confess Jesus Christ as their Lord and still live the way they did before they were born again. They are still in love with Egypt. They love to recall what a good time they had before they were saved, "Man, I used to get so high and so drunk; and we had the greatest parties." They forget about the hangovers. They forget about the damage they did to their souls, to their bodies, to their families, and to their future. They're still in love with the world and still blinded to its lies.

The Bible says emphatically:

> *Love not the world, neither the things that are in the world. If any man love the world, the love of the Father is not in him. For all that is in the world, the lust of the flesh, and the lust of the eyes, and the pride of life, is not of the Father, but is of the world. And the world passeth away, and the lust thereof: but he that doeth the will of God abideth for ever.*   1 John 2:15-17

If you are still in love with Egypt, then you're not ready to go to war for God. Jesus said:

> *If any man will come after me, let him deny himself, and take up his cross daily, and follow me.*   Luke 9:23

Denying yourself means to crucify the fleshly tendencies, and the second step is to follow after the voice of the Spirit. Paul knew what it was to crucify the flesh; he said that he died *"daily"* (see 1 Corinthians 15:31).

Paul was saying that he put to death the works of the flesh every day. He took the sword of the Spirit, which is the Word of God, and circumcised his heart daily. Why? Because he knew that if he went to war with his flesh ruling his spirit, he would surely be defeated.

One of the reasons the giants of Canaan so greatly feared the Israelite warriors was that the Israelites were circumcised. That was very significant for them. They were a people set apart. They had the mark of God on them. Everyone knew it, and every enemy feared them because of it. Unless you are willing to be identified with the Lord and to bear His seal upon your life, you will be no different than others around you.

Circumcision today may mean cutting away television time or passing up certain meals. It may mean that you can be found in church instead of in some shopping mall. It may mean that you will be on your face praying instead of playing golf three times a week.

Some might say, "Man, that sounds like a miserable existence."

Well, it could be a miserable existence if you chose to do those things without first cutting away the flesh. But when you have cut away the flesh, those things become secondary to you and you are willing and ready to do anything that will bring you closer to God and His will for your life:

> *And the children of Israel encamped in Gilgal, and kept the passover on the fourteenth day of*

the month at even in the plains of Jericho. And
they did eat of the old corn of the land on the
morrow after the passover, unleavened cakes,
and parched corn in the selfsame day.

Joshua 5:10-11

The third thing the children of Israel did after crossing the Jordan River was to celebrate the Passover. The Passover was another form of remembrance, like the memorial they built; but its prophetic significance concerned reconciliation and fellowship. It spoke of the power of the blood to cover sins. It signified God's forgiveness and His mercy, and it drew His people into a closer place of fellowship with Him.

The Passover also reminded the Israelites of God's supernatural protection for their households when the Death Angel passed over Egypt. The firstborn in every Egyptian home died that night, but the families of the Israelites were safe behind the blood they had applied to the door posts and lintels of their humble houses. Not one Israelite son died. It was important to remind themselves of these events as they now prepared to go into battle.

God's Word declares:

But seek ye first the kingdom of God, and his
righteousness; and all these things shall be
added unto you.   Matthew 6:33

By celebrating the Passover, the children of Israel were saying, "God, we're seeking You first in our lives. We want to do Your will, and we want Your righteousness." Because they were faithful to do this, God was able to work on their behalf and to supply their every need.

It is time to celebrate a Passover in our own hearts, time to affirm to ourselves and to others that we are redeemed from the curse of the Law:

> *Christ hath redeemed us from the curse of the law, being made a curse for us.*
> Galatians 3:13

It is time to remember all that God has done in our own lives and time to push aside all murmuring and all complaining. I will be reminded of God's goodness to me and to my family, of His safekeeping, and of the miracles He has done in the past to keep me safe and fulfill His promises to me. Assured of His protection, I am ready to go forth and defeat giants.

When the children of Israel had finished building their memorial, had finished circumcising all their males, and had celebrated the Passover, God confirmed His presence by blessing them:

> *And the manna ceased on the morrow after they had eaten of the old corn of the land; neither had the children of Israel manna any more; but they did eat of the fruit of the land of Canaan that year.*
> Joshua 5:12

That may not sound like much of a blessing to some people. It would frighten a lot of Christians.

They would be afraid that they were backsliding, losing their place of fellowship with the Lord. But God revealed His favor upon the lives of His people by causing the manna to cease — after forty years. He was not withdrawing His hand of blessing from His people; He was leading them into new blessings. The fact that the manna ceased did not represent a step backward, but a step forward. The manna had been wonderful, but now they would eat of the goodness of the land: *"But they did eat of the fruit of the land of Canaan that year."*

This is an important truth. When we begin to possess new territory for God, He may supply for us in new ways. He may work for us through new miracles. We don't need manna when we have a land flowing with milk and honey. That didn't diminish the importance of the miracle of the manna, but milk and honey was better.

Elijah had nothing to fear when the brook dried up and the ravens ceased to come. God had prepared a widow to feed him. And when the widow's barrel was exhausted, the rains came and the land produced once again.

This is no time to moan and complain. It is time to rejoice. We may be leaving the old, but we are moving into the new. We may be leaving some wonderful experiences, but we are moving on toward greater experiences. With God, it is never backward but always forward; never less but always more; never down but always up.

Get ready to eat the fruits of your new blessings, your inheritance. Get ready to eat of the fatness of your Promised Land. Get ready to partake of the goodness of your prophetic promise. If you have properly prepared for possession, you have every right to expect God to move on your behalf.

Chapter 7

The Battle for Possession

And it came to pass, when Joshua was by Jericho, that he lifted up his eyes and looked, and, behold, there stood a man over against him with his sword drawn in his hand: and Joshua went unto him, and said unto him, Art thou for us, or for our adversaries? And he said, Nay; but as captain of the host of the LORD am I now come. And Joshua fell on his face to the earth, and did worship, and said unto him, What saith my lord unto his servant? And the captain of the LORD's host said unto Joshua, Loose thy shoe from off thy foot; for the place whereon thou standest is holy. And Joshua did so.   Joshua 5:13-15

The children of Israel had cast off the grasshopper mentality, sanctified themselves, and crossed over the Jordan. They had erected the memorial, circumcised the men, and celebrated the Passover. Now, it was time to proceed toward possession. All that led up to this moment was wonderful, but it was just the prelude, just the introduction. The best was yet to come. They had been blessed, but they hadn't conquered anything yet and hadn't taken possession of any land for the Lord.

Sad to say, many people never get further than this in their Christian walk. They are still in the preliminary stages, still in the introduction, and are missing the best of what God has to offer. They have not yet possessed their prophetic promises.

The goal of the Christian life is not thanksgiving or celebration or circumcision. It is possession. Everything else leads us to possession, but everything else does not equal possession. It is time to fight for what is rightfully ours. Apparently, the Lord felt that Israel was now ready to go into battle; and He was prepared to lead them.

Some believe that *"the captain of the* Lord's *host"* in this passage was an angel, but notice Joshua's reaction to him. He *"fell to the earth, and did worship."* We are not to worship angels, and there is no account in the Scriptures of any man doing it. This was no ordinary angel; this was the Lord Himself, come to lead His people into battle. He was there waiting for them when they got across the Jordan. They didn't leave

Him on the other side in the wilderness. He wasn't restricted to the old experiences. He is God of the new, as well as God of the old. He was with us yesterday; He is with us today; and He will be with us tomorrow.

And He is not a God of emergencies. He did not wait to manifest His presence until the heat of the battle and the moment of emergency. He was there from the very beginning. He is with us always and everywhere. He was not waiting to be called upon at the last moment in time of desperation. He would go before them and lead them into battle.

Why is it that the Church has felt so lonely and helpless in battle these days? Why is it that we get the impression that we are all alone on the front lines? We have been *hoping* that we are doing the right thing, *hoping* to make the right moves, *hoping* to act at the right time. But we're not sure sometimes. We need to get the revelation that God is preparing the way for us. David had that revelation. He said:

> *Yea, though I walk through the valley of the shadow of death, I will fear no evil: for thou art with me; thy rod and thy staff they comfort me. Thou preparest a table before me in the presence of mine enemies: thou anointest my head with oil; my cup runneth over.* Psalms 23:4-5

Zerubbabel received that revelation. God told him:

> *Not by might, nor by power, but by my spirit, saith the* Lord *of hosts.* Zechariah 4:6

Paul had that revelation. He declared:

> *Nay, in all these things we are more than con-*
> *querors through him that loved us.*
>
> Romans 8:37

When we make up our minds to move out of the wilderness and into the Promised Land, the Lord will be waiting there with His sword in hand to lead us forth into the battle:

> *Now Jericho was straitly shut up because of the*
> *children of Israel: none went out, and none came*
> *in. And the* LORD *said unto Joshua, See, I have*
> *given into thine hand Jericho, and the king*
> *thereof, and the mighty men of valour.*
>
> Joshua 6:1-2

Jericho looked very much as the first spies had reported it nearly forty years before. If Jericho hadn't changed, what had changed? Why could Joshua and his generation take Jericho when Moses and his generation could not? We already know that the mentality of the Hebrews had changed, but the mentality of the people of Jericho had also changed dramatically. Before, they had laughed at the idea of being conquered by a group of wandering slaves. Now, their attitude had changed.

When the children of Israel became disgusted with wandering in the wilderness and decided to rise up in God and possess what belonged to them, when they got tired of eating manna and longed to eat the fruit of their own land, when they realized who they were and what they had been promised, it influenced not only their own thinking but the thinking of the enemy as well. When Joshua and his people realized that they were children of God, when they decided to believe His Word, when they became identified as His chosen, when they made up their minds to cross the Jordan and enter into their Promised Land, when they chose to stand up against the giants who were inhabiting their property, then God went before them and placed fear in the hearts of their enemies. The people of Jericho were suddenly terrified.

The Church of today has lost sight of who should be afraid of whom. We see another documentary on Satanism or read about more violence in the newspaper, we hear another report about the rising interest rates and the troubled economy, and what do we do? We run and shut up our gates against the enemy in the *hope* that he won't be able to break through. The Church of the twentieth century has become a spineless, spiritual jellyfish being squashed beneath the feet of sickness, poverty, confusion, fear, frustration, and death.

Instead, we should be believing what the Word of God says:

> *Ye are of God, little children, and have overcome them: because greater is he that is in you, than he that is in the world.* 1 John 4:4

We have believed that if we can just endure to the end, someday, somehow we'll receive a crown. But this is not the victorious Church of Scripture. This is not the army that can defeat every enemy. This is not the group of triumphant ones who will take Jericho. The Church needs backbone if we are to possess what God has promised us.

You and I must wake up to the fact that Jesus Christ is truly the King of kings and the Lord of lords. He has prepared the way for us, and He is going before us into battle. When we take hold of this revelation and become transformed by the renewing of our minds, we will rise up in God and the strongholds of Satan will quickly shut their doors in fear.

When God's people rise up in power, ready to do battle, Satan will fortify himself in his stronghold and hope to "fake us out." But it will not work because God has already given us the victory.

Jericho was the border stronghold of the Canaanites; and, as such, it had to fall. The Israelites could not simply pass it by and hope to conquer other territories. They must turn Jericho into a stronghold for God.

God also has his strongholds. Some churches and some ministries, as well as some men and women of God, are mighty, positive, spiritual strongholds for God's Kingdom. We have strongholds built up in the north, south, east, and west; and Satan wants to tear them down. In some cases, he has succeeded. We have seen a few spiritual fortresses fall lately. But don't despair; in the end, the victory will be ours because we are on the winning side:

> *The kingdoms of this world are become the kingdoms of our Lord, and of his Christ; and he shall reign for ever and ever.* Revelation 11:15

God promised Joshua three things: *"Jericho, the king thereof, and the mighty men of valour." "Jericho"* is the enemy stronghold. *"The king thereof"* is Satan himself. And *"the mighty men of valour"* represent the demons and their vile activities. God said He would give them all into our hands. We have nothing to fear from evil men, from Satan himself, or from the hordes of demons at work in the world.

This is not our war; it's God's war. The enemy has stepped onto God's turf; for when he decided to take on God's people, he decided to take on God. And God didn't raise the white flag of surrender. He issued a declaration of war.

God is not pleased that His people have allowed the enemy to build strongholds on His property. He wants us to rise up and take our land because He has already given us the victory. Jesus fought the battle for us two thousand years ago when He stormed the gates of hell:

> *Wherefore he saith, When he ascended up on high, he led captivity captive, and gave gifts unto men. Now that he ascended, what is it but*

> *that he also descended first into the lower parts*
> *of the earth?*   Ephesians 4:8-9

Jesus wasn't sneaking around, afraid of His own shadow. He strode up and down the corridors of the underworld and said, "I will take back everything you have stolen from My people, and I will place the keys to your stronghold in their hands."

Jesus tells us what He accomplished that day:

> *I am he that liveth, and was dead; and, behold, I*
> *am alive for evermore, Amen; and have the keys*
> *of hell and of death.*   Revelation 1:18

Since we are joint heirs with Christ, everything He has belongs to us. So rejoice! We own the keys to Satan's strongholds.

Don't feel sorry for the Canaanites. They were evil people. Among them were idolaters, witches, fortune-tellers, diviners, occultists, and every other wicked thing you could imagine. These were not innocent people, and God didn't want them living in His land. So, He determined to evict them and to give the land to His people. And He wasn't pleased when it took forty years more to redeem His property. But this was not just a battle between the nation of Israel and the squatters on their land. This was God's holy war. And God has never lost a battle. It doesn't matter what the odds are. He always wins.

At a later time when evil inhabitants of the land came against the Israelites, God once again reminded them that the battle was His, not theirs:

> *And he said, Hearken ye, all Judah, and ye inhabitants of Jerusalem, and thou king Jehoshaphat, Thus saith the LORD unto you, Be not afraid nor dismayed by reason of this great multitude; for the battle is not yours, but God's.*
> 2 Chronicles 20:15

When God is fighting for you, there is never a reason to be afraid or dismayed. The devil and all the demons of hell cannot possibly hurt you as long as God is on your side:

> *To morrow go ye down against them: behold, they come up by the cliff of Ziz; and ye shall find them at the end of the brook, before the wilderness of Jeruel.* 2 Chronicles 20:16

God doesn't fight blindly. He knows where to find the enemy:

> *Ye shall not need to fight in this battle: set yourselves, stand ye still, and see the salvation of the LORD with you, O Judah and Jerusalem: fear not, nor be dismayed; to morrow go out against them: for the LORD will be with you.*
> 2 Chronicles 20:17

The men of war didn't have to fight. All they had to do was *"stand still"* and watch *"the salvation of the LORD"*:

> *And Jehoshaphat bowed his head with his face to
> the ground: and all Judah and the inhabitants of
> Jerusalem fell before the* LORD, *worshipping the*
> LORD. *And the Levites, of the children of the
> Kohathites, and of the children of the Korhites,
> stood up to praise the* LORD *God of Israel with a
> loud voice on high.*   2 Chronicles 20:18-19

What were these men doing? They were offering
thanksgiving to God — even before they saw victory
— just like Israel did at Jericho:

> *And they rose early in the morning, and went
> forth into the wilderness of Tekoa: and as they
> went forth, Jehoshaphat stood and said, Hear
> me, O Judah, and ye inhabitants of Jerusalem;
> Believe in the* LORD *your God, so shall ye be
> established; believe his prophets, so shall ye
> prosper.*   2 Chronicles 20:20

This is a very important point. When you listen to
the voice of God's true prophets, then you will prosper — physically, emotionally, financially, and
spiritually. But if you go to a church where the pastor
pats you on the back and says, "It's okay to live like
the devil. Just come fill my pews every Sunday," and
he doesn't equip you with the armor of God, then
you will not have the power to take back your property from the devil. You may get just enough to
survive; but you won't get enough to prosper.

Find a church where a true prophet of God is ministering — a man who hears from God and declares His Word — and work with that man to see God's will accomplished. This will assure your prosperity:

> *And when he had consulted with the people, he appointed singers unto the* LORD, *and that should praise the beauty of holiness, as they went out before the army, and to say, Praise the* LORD; *for his mercy endureth for ever.*
>
> 2 Chronicles 20:21

Two elements were of utmost importance in battle: praise and obedience.

Logistically, they may have thought it was more sensible to praise God while they were destroying the enemy or after the battle was won. But God told them to send the praisers out first. Because the praisers had no weapons, it may have seemed unfair and unwise to place them in harm's way. But God said to send them first, and Israel obeyed:

> *And when they began to sing and to praise, the* LORD *set ambushments against the children of Ammon, Moab, and mount Seir, which were come against Judah; and they were smitten. For the children of Ammon and Moab stood up against the inhabitants of mount Seir, utterly to slay and destroy them: and when they had made an end of the inhabitants of Seir, every one helped to destroy another.*
>
> 2 Chronicles 20:22-23

A wonderful thing happened when Israel honored God and *"began to sing and praise."* The enemies turned on themselves and killed each other.

It can happen today in the same way. The devil will turn on himself, and we can stand by and watch *the salvation of the Lord.* But first, God is demanding of us a harvest of souls. There are people out there in the enemy's camp whom God wants to reach. They may be unlovely and unlovable, but God has His hand on their lives. It is up to you and me to deliver them before they are destroyed.

Rise up. The battle is not ours, but the Lord's. He will surely give us the victory. He will cause the enemy to defeat his own cause:

> *And when Judah came toward the watch tower in the wilderness, they looked unto the multitude, and, behold, they were dead bodies fallen to the earth, and none escaped.*
>
> 2 Chronicles 20:24

The *"watch tower"* here is the stronghold. The devil's strongholds are always in *"the wilderness."* When the men of Judah got close to this stronghold, they found that all its defenders were already dead. There was nothing more to do but rejoice and gather up the spoils:

> *And when Jehoshaphat and his people came to take away the spoil of them, they found among*

> *them in abundance both riches with the dead*
> *bodies, and precious jewels, which they stripped*
> *off for themselves, more than they could carry*
> *away: and they were three days in gathering of*
> *the spoil, it was so much.*
>
> 2 Chronicles 20:25

It took three days to carry away all the spoils of battle. What a miracle! The Bible says:

> *... the wealth of the sinner is laid up for the just.*
> Proverbs 13:22

It's time for the people of God to start gathering up what is theirs. It's time to gather up your riches of joy; it's time to reap your riches of health; it's time to receive your riches of prosperity; it's time to take up your riches of salvation for your family. You won't do it all by the efforts of your flesh; you'll do it by learning to praise God and allowing Him to fight your battle.

David learned very early in life to let God fight his battles. By the time he faced Goliath, he had learned his lesson well.

Goliath was no pushover. The entire army of Israel was in fear because of him and his exploits. The men were surprised when David agreed to fight the giant. They hadn't yet learned David's secret. David looked at Goliath not as a giant to be feared, but as an *"uncircumcised Philistine"* who did not have God's mark upon him and who was, therefore, no match for

God's chosen people. As God's enemy, Goliath had no authority to defy the armies of Israel:

> *And David spake to the men that stood by him, saying, What shall be done to the man that killeth this Philistine, and taketh away the reproach from Israel? for who is this uncircumcised Philistine, that he should defy the armies of the living God?* 1 Samuel 17:26

David wasn't afraid of a giant. He wasn't afraid of an uncircumcised Philistine. He knew the power of God to deliver; and because of that, he was ready and even eager to fight the giant.

We need to stay so full of the Spirit of God that we will not be intimidated by the thought of being sent out against drug addiction or AIDS or any other enemy of God. When we learn about the difficult cases, we should be eager to take them on, eager to see the hand of God revealed in our behalf. We have nothing to fear.

Saul offered David his own armor, but David knew he couldn't fight Goliath wearing somebody else's mantle. He needed to stand against the giant in his own anointing. And when David went out to fight the Philistine, Goliath was offended:

> *And when the Philistine looked about, and saw David, he disdained him: for he was but a youth, and ruddy, and of a fair countenance.*
> 1 Samuel 17:42

The devil may laugh when he sees us coming, but he won't laugh long:

> *Then said David to the Philistine, Thou comest to me with a sword, and with a spear, and with a shield: but I come to thee in the name of the LORD of hosts, the God of the armies of Israel, whom thou hast defied. This day will the LORD deliver thee into mine hand; and I will smite thee, and take thine head from thee; and I will give the carcases of the host of the Philistines this day unto the fowls of the air, and to the wild beasts of the earth; that all the earth may know that there is a God in Israel. And all this assembly shall know that the LORD saveth not with sword and spear: for the battle is the LORD's, and he will give you into our hands.* 1 Samuel 17:45-47

The battle is the Lord's. David wasn't afraid of Goliath's spear. He knew that no giant was a match for Almighty God. He prophesied to Goliath that he wouldn't survive the battle. Some people just want to have a sparring match with Satan; but David intended to kill his tormentor, once and for all:

> *And it came to pass, when the Philistine arose, and came, and drew nigh to meet David, that David hasted, and ran toward the army to meet the Philistine.* 1 Samuel 17:48

David ran to meet the giant. He didn't try to sneak around the back way. He ran forward in Goliath's sight. He wasn't afraid. He knew that a battle fought in the name of the Lord could not be lost. And the rest is history.

Goliath was doomed to failure from the minute he defied the armies of God. In the end, he fell to a small shepherd boy, and David's victory that day turned the tide for the entire nation of Israel. Stand up in the name of the Lord and give Him the opportunity to turn the tide of your nation as well.

War is not something we like. If we could, most of us would avoid confrontation. It is never pleasant. But God shows us in His Word, that there is a time for war:

> *To every thing there is a season, and a time to every purpose under the heaven:*
> *A time to love, and a time to hate; a time of war, and a time of peace.* Ecclesiastes 3:1 & 8

We have just come through a long period of peace in the history of the Church; and, in my opinion, we are approaching a time of unprecedented war. This period of peace has been wonderful because we have been able to rebuild and replenish our souls. We have spent time strengthening our spirits and stock-piling knowledge. This generation probably knows more about the Word of God than any preceding generation. We know who we are in Christ Jesus, and we've learned how to maintain victory in our circumstances. But the time for peace is now over, and it is time for us to march into our land and drive out the giants who are living there. We must now possess what is rightfully ours.

Attempting to ignore the fact that battle is imminent will not change anything. We can no longer ignore it; war is inevitable. Just as battles and wars in diverse locations across the planet fill our nightly newscasts, war is heating up in the spiritual realm as well. All hell is about to break loose.

This war will be for eternal values. Therefore, it is not just a matter of life and death; but a matter of eternal life and eternal death.

I call upon those who seem to be paralyzed with fear by the approaching storm. Saints of God, arise. Go forth to battle.

Why is it that much of the Church does not want to face the reality of war? Is it because we have become too comfortable and don't want to be disturbed? Do you think that just because you have opted not to enter the fray, that Satan will leave you alone? You may indeed be his next target. You may be scheduled to become his next victim. You don't have the option of saying you will not participate. We're all in this together. If you sit back and do nothing, Satan will invade your space and make an all-out attack on you.

Gang violence doesn't seem to affect most of us — when we only read about it in the newspaper. It is only when our own family is terrorized, brutalized, raped, or murdered that the problem hits home.

Most of us can ignore the drug problem — until one of our own children becomes addicted to cocaine or until a loved one dies of a drug overdose.

Abortion doesn't seem to affect most of us — until it's your own daughter returning from the abortion clinic.

Alcoholism seems to affect only old men who sleep in doorways — until a close friend can't cope with the pressures of life and turns to the bottle.

You can't ignore this battle any longer. You can't afford to stand on the sidelines any longer. You can't claim ignorance any longer. You can't deny that this thing involves you and your family any longer. We are at war. Take your position and fight with the rest of us.

During the early part of World War II, military intelligence warned us, over and over again, that the bombing of Pearl Harbor was probable. The American military chose to ignore those warnings, and thousands of lives were lost because we failed to prepare. In the same way, God is trying to warn His people of impending war; but most of us are ignoring His warnings. Satan is waging a war to destroy your marriage, to destroy your morality, to steal your children and your health, and to control everything that you hold dear in life.

Jesus said:

> *The thief cometh not, but for to steal, and to kill, and to destroy: I am come that they might have life, and that they might have it more abundantly.*   John 10:10

We could avoid many of the tragedies in life if we would wake up, recognize that we are at war, and get ready to do battle. It's your choice. We can wait until we're attacked and sinking in the harbor to try to fight; or we can rise up now, cross over into victory, and possess the abundant life that God says we can have.

Satan is not waiting. While we are preparing our picket signs, he is storming our strongholds. Stop trying to use the weapons of the flesh and learn to use spiritual weapons:

> *(For the weapons of our warfare are not carnal, but mighty through God to the pulling down of strong holds;)*　　　　2 Corinthians 10:4

Learn to use the Word of God:

> *No weapon that is formed against thee shall prosper.*　　　　Isaiah 54:17

> *Behold, I give unto you power to tread on serpents and scorpions, and over all the power of the enemy: and nothing shall by any means hurt you.*　　　　Luke 10:19

Neither your carnal intellect nor your fleshly abilities can help you conquer the enemies in your land. It is only by the revelation of the Holy Spirit that you can be victorious, and that revelation comes through the knowledge of God's Word.

Stand on it. Use it like the sword it is. Start believing and acting upon the knowledge you have gained during times of peace. Put your knowledge into action. That's the difference between the medical student and the surgeon. That's the difference between victory and defeat. That's the difference between a grasshopper generation of survivors and a new generation of possessors.

Start believing that you are what God's Word says you are:

> *But ye are a chosen generation, a royal priesthood, an holy nation, a peculiar people; that ye should shew forth the praises of him who hath called you out of darkness into his marvellous light:*   1 Peter 2:9

> *Ye are the salt of the earth.*   Matthew 5:13

> *Ye are the light of the world.*   Matthew 5:14

> *What? know ye not that your body is the temple of the Holy Ghost which is in you.*
>   1 Corinthians 6:19

> *And hath made us kings and priests unto God and his Father.*   Revelation 1:6

Start believing that you can have what God's Word says you can have:

> *There shall no evil befall thee, neither shall any plague come nigh thy dwelling.*
>   Psalms 91:10

Train up a child in the way he should go: and when he is old, he will not depart from it.
                                                    Proverbs 22:6

Learning to use the Word of God will renew your mind in the Spirit:

And be not conformed to this world: but be ye transformed by the renewing of your mind, that ye may prove what is that good, and acceptable, and perfect, will of God.   Romans 12:2

A renewed mind will no longer be trapped in a mind-set which actually opposes God's plan for your life. A renewed mind will recognize that you don't have to stay poor forever. A renewed mind will know that just because you have always been sick in the past doesn't mean you have to remain sick all your life. Through using God's Word as an implement, you can actually put on the mind of Christ:

Let this mind be in you, which was also in Christ Jesus: Philippians 2:5

Christ is the embodiment of God's Word; and when we renew our minds to God's Word, then we can have the brilliance and the power of Jesus Christ working through us so that we can go forth in the battle for possession.

Chapter 8

The Key to Possession

And the Lord *said unto Joshua, See, I have given into thine hand Jericho, and the king thereof, and the mighty men of valour. And ye shall compass the city, all ye men of war, and go round about the city once. Thus shalt thou do six days. And seven priests shall bear before the ark seven trumpets of rams' horns: and the seventh day ye shall compass the city seven times, and the priests shall blow with the trumpets. And it shall come to pass, that when they make a long blast with the ram's horn, and when ye hear the sound of the trumpet, all the people shall shout*

with a great shout; and the wall of the city shall
fall down flat, and the people shall ascend up
every man straight before him.   Joshua 6:2-5

Notice that God gave the battle plan only to
Joshua. He didn't tell Eleazer and the priests; He
didn't tell Caleb; He didn't tell the soldiers; He didn't
tell the people. He told Joshua, and Joshua relayed
the information to the rest of Israel. This was a prophetic foretelling that only Jesus Christ Himself is
given the battle plan for our day, and Jesus is relay-
ing the information to you and to me.

Joshua issued God's orders for battle, and everybody followed his instructions to the letter. Everyone
obeyed Joshua. Obedience was their key to possession, and it is still a valid key to victory today. All
that God requires of His armies in any battle is simply to obey His orders.

One of the problems we face in the Church today is
that only a few people accept the fact that God knows
more about winning battles than we do. "Let's talk
about it," they say. So everybody asks everybody
else what he or she thinks about God's instructions.
And we're so busy listening to everyone's opinion
(or everyone's complaint) that we can't hear the
voice of God.

The biggest problem Moses had with the children
of Israel in the desert was that they were always murmuring and complaining. They were always talking
about what was wrong. That's a major problem today, as well.

When we stop complaining and start listening to the voice of God, our vocabulary changes and we start to say what God says. When the devil tells me, "Bagwell, you can't make it," I say: *"Greater is he that is in [me], than he that is in the world."* When sickness tries to overtake my body, I say: *"Beloved, I wish above all things that thou mayest prosper and be in health, even as thy soul prospereth."* When the adversary shouts, "You're a loser," I rise up and declare: *"And they overcame him by the blood of the Lamb, and by the word of their testimony."* My confession helps me to become transformed because I am renewing my mind and faith is created in my heart when I hear God's Word.

The Israelites became transformed from "maintainers" into conquerors by the renewing of their minds. I doubt that they stood any taller physically than their fathers of forty years before. The number of soldiers was about the same. In the flesh, they were the same people; but in the spirit, they were transformed into mighty warriors.

Have you ever noticed that maintainers are always murmuring, while possessors are always speaking God's Word? I believe that's why God instructed the soldiers to be silent:

> *And Joshua had commanded the people, saying, Ye shall not shout, nor make any noise with your voice, neither shall any word proceed out of your mouth, until the day I bid you shout; then shall ye shout.*   Joshua 6:10

To the natural mind, this would have seemed fool-ish, but what seems foolish to us is counted as faith when we are obeying God's commands. Jesus said:

> *Not every one that saith unto me, Lord, Lord, shall enter into the kingdom of heaven; but he that doeth the will of my Father which is in heaven. Many will say to me in that day, Lord, Lord, have we not prophesied in thy name? and in thy name have cast out devils? and in thy name done many wonderful works? And then will I profess unto them, I never knew you: depart from me, ye that work iniquity.*
>   Matthew 7:21-23

Many people have a form of righteousness; but if it is not in line with God's Word, then it is not moti-vated by faith. And we know that we cannot please Him without faith:

> *Without faith it is impossible to please him.*
>   Hebrews 11:6

Too many people think they can do things better than God can, and they take their battles into their own hands. That's not faith; that's flesh. After a while, they become frustrated and begin to fight with fleshly anger. But that's not God's way. God requires obedience in faith.

There comes a time when we need to be silent and obey the voice of God. I'm ready to be quiet if that is

His command; or I will shout if that is His command. I'm willing to dance or to stand in the gap or to fast or to pray. I am willing to do what He bids me to do because He knows best for me. "Just command me, Lord," is the cry of my heart.

If my orders are to walk, then I'm going to walk — no more and no less. And that takes faith because God tests us. Look what happened the first day the Israelites marched around Jericho. Nothing!

What happened on the second day? Nothing!

They followed the same instructions the third day and the fourth, fifth, and sixth days. And still nothing happened.

It's easy to have faith if you receive your answer the same day you pray. But when you obey God and nothing seems to be happening, that's a true test of faith.

What happened on the seventh day?

> *And it came to pass on the seventh day, that they rose early about the dawning of the day, and compassed the city after the same manner seven times: only on that day they compassed the city seven times. And it came to pass at the seventh time, when the priests blew with the trumpets, Joshua said unto the people, Shout; for the LORD hath given you the city.*   Joshua 6:15-16

The seventh day they marched seven times as much. You see, obedience is not always doing just what you've been doing. Sometimes it *is* doing what you've been doing, and sometimes it means going the extra mile. We want miracles on our own conditions, but they don't come that way. We must obey God, whether it is convenient or not. We must obey God, even when it's disagreeable — to our schedules, to our energy levels, to our comfort zones — because miracles don't come on our convenience level. They come on our obedience level.

The Israelites obeyed God and marched seven times as much on the seventh day as they had on the previous six days. Still, everything seemed to be against them. The gates of Jericho were still locked; the windows were still shut; and the guards were still in their places on the walls. Nothing had changed, except that God's people had fully obeyed Him. And that makes all the difference in the world. God works for us — when we obey Him fully.

This is why it is so important to know that we are obeying the Lord and not some man's doctrine. The Apostle Paul said:

> *For if the trumpet give an uncertain sound, who shall prepare himself to the battle?*
> 1 Corinthians 14:8

I realize the context here concerns speaking in tongues, but I believe the truth is applicable to this prophetic message. If everybody hears a different message, then we won't be united in a single purpose and we will not succeed in possessing our Promised Land.

Too many Christians are trying to watch the signs of the times instead of keeping their eyes in God's Word and listening to the voice of His Spirit. Isaiah prophesied to the generation who would trust God to deliver their enemies into their hands:

> *Open ye the gates, that the righteous nation which keepeth the truth may enter in. Thou wilt keep him in perfect peace, whose mind is stayed on thee: because he trusteth in thee. Trust ye in the* LORD *for ever: for in the* LORD *JEHOVAH is everlasting strength: For he bringeth down them that dwell on high; the lofty city, he layeth it low; he layeth it low, even to the ground; he bringeth it even to the dust.* Isaiah 26:2-5

> *Cry aloud, spare not, lift up thy voice like a trumpet, and shew my people their transgression, and the house of Jacob their sins.*
> Isaiah 58:1

This is a call to battle: "Sound the battle cry. Put on your armor. Cry out loud and don't hold back!" That means don't water down your zeal; don't dilute or pollute your determination to win. Lift up your voice like a trumpet.

In the Old Testament, the sound of the trumpet and the number and length of the blasts conveyed various messages to the children of Israel. For the trumpets were a means of conveying God's orders to such a large company.

On this day, V-day at Jericho, the people were listening closely for the signal to go forth to battle. When they heard it, they lifted up their voices in a mighty victory shout which historians call "ear-splitting," a Holy Ghost shout that caused the walls of Jericho to come crashing to the ground.

Get your ear attuned to the sound of God's trumpet:

> *Also I set watchmen over you, saying, Hearken to the sound of the trumpet.*   Jeremiah 6:17

> *Blow ye the trumpet in Zion, and sound an alarm in my holy mountain: let all the inhabitants of the land tremble: for the day of the* Lord *cometh, for it is nigh at hand;*   Joel 2:1

> *And the* Lord *shall utter his voice before his army: for his camp is very great: for he is strong that executeth his word: for the day of the* Lord *is great and very terrible; and who can abide it?*
> Joel 2:11

> *Blow the trumpet in Zion, sanctify a fast, call a solemn assembly:*   Joel 2:15

God's trumpet has a dual purpose. It not only incites His people to march into battle, but it also strikes terror in the hearts of His enemies. And soon, some very special trumpets will sound:

> *But in the days of the voice of the seventh angel,
> when he shall begin to sound, the mystery of
> God should be finished, as he hath declared to his
> servants the prophets.* Revelation 10:7

"The seventh angel" here refers to a messenger.
God's messengers, His prophets, are sounding His
trumpet in this day.

What will happen when God's people hear His
trumpet? *"When he shall begin to sound, the mystery of
God should be finished."* God is going to show us a
mystery:

> *But as it is written, Eye hath not seen, nor ear
> heard, neither have entered into the heart of
> man, the things which God hath prepared for
> them that love him. But God hath revealed them
> unto us by his Spirit: for the Spirit searcheth all
> things, yea, the deep things of God.*
> 1 Corinthians 2:9-10

God is revealing to us the wonderful things He has
prepared for us in these last days; but we must be
listening closely to the voice of His Spirit, or we will
miss it. And we must obey Him fully if we are to see
His glory manifested:

> *And the seventh angel sounded; and there were
> great voices in heaven, saying, The kingdoms of
> this world are become the kingdoms of our Lord,
> and of his Christ; and he shall reign for ever and
> ever.* Revelation 11:15

This trumpet will signal the final battle. We're not going to win this skirmish and lose ground next month. We're going to win once and for all, and the Lord Jesus Christ will reign in our Promised Land forever and ever. Hallelujah!

Learn total obedience, for it is the key to possession.

Chapter 9

The First Hindrance to Possession: Sin

And it came to pass at the seventh time, when the priests blew with the trumpets, Joshua said unto the people, Shout; for the LORD hath given you the city. And the city shall be accursed, even it, and all that are therein, to the LORD: only Rahab the harlot shall live, she and all that are with her in the house, because she hid the messengers that we sent. And ye, in any wise keep yourselves from the accursed thing, lest ye make yourselves accursed, when ye take of the accursed thing, and make the camp of Israel a curse, and trouble it. But all the silver, and gold,

*and vessels of brass and iron, are consecrated
unto the* LORD: *they shall come into the treasury
of the* LORD.   Joshua 6:16-19

God cut a covenant with Israel concerning the city
of Jericho. His part of the covenant was to give the
city of Jericho into the hands of the Israelites; and
their part of the covenant was to turn over to the
House of the Lord all the silver, gold, brass, and iron
they recovered as spoil from the enemy. What a
simple agreement! All of the plunder was to be relin-
quished to the Tabernacle to be used as God saw fit,
and none of it was to go to any individual.

There was, however, a man named Achan who
decided that nobody would miss just a little of that
booty; and he took *"two hundred shekels of silver, a
wedge of gold, and a Babylonish garment."* Compared to
the vast amount of spoils found in the entire city of
Jericho that would seem like a very small amount.
Who would care about that? Yet God's instructions
had been very clear.

I don't know why people have such a hard time
understanding directions. God means what He says.
You can't afford to hedge with His instructions.

Achan stole a few small items and brought a curse
upon the whole nation:

*But the children of Israel committed a trespass
in the accursed thing: for Achan, the son of
Carmi, the son of Zabdi, the son of Zerah, of the*

> *tribe of Judah, took of the accursed thing: and the*
> *anger of the* LORD *was kindled against the chil-*
> *dren of Israel.* Joshua 7:1

The whole congregation of the children of Israel had to pay for one man's sin. And that may not seem fair. The others did nothing wrong, yet everyone had to pay. We must realize that the Church is a family and that every member of the family is accountable for the actions of other brothers and sisters. We can no longer push off our responsibility on others. It doesn't matter who sins; that sin affects us all.

As members of the community, we must accept our responsibility. The drugs and violence and teen pregnancies in our cities are not just the mayor's responsibility or the sheriff's responsibility. They are *our* responsibility too. The Scriptures declare:

> *And whether one member suffer, all the members*
> *suffer with it.* 1 Corinthians 12:26

We have whitewashed and spiritualized this passage so long that when we read about tragedies in the newspaper, they seem like just another statistic, totally unrelated to our world. And we don't really feel the suffering connected with them.

The Church today is closing its eyes to a lot of suffering and a lot of sin. But the day is approaching in which we had better wake up, or God will awaken us:

*And the times of this ignorance God winked at;
but now commandeth all men every where to
repent:*   Acts 17:30

The Church winks too much at sin. We accept too
much in the name of "grace" or "forgiveness." When
our brothers or sisters sin, we look the other way. We
have become a tolerant generation. We've winked at
sin so long that we now have a higher percentage of
teenage pregnancies than any other past generation.
We've winked at sin so long that we now have the
highest divorce rate in the history of our nation.
We've winked at sin so long that we now have the
highest rate of alcoholism in history. We have gang
violence, drugs in grade school, jealousy, murmuring, backbiting, and murder — all because the
church has been winking at sin.

Instead of taking responsibility and being accountable, the church, has preached nice little sermonettes
which say, "I'm okay. You're okay. He's okay. She's
okay. We're okay. It's all okay."

Pastors must step forward in boldness and declare
God's truth. They must be more concerned with the
quality of their members' walk with God than they
are with filling the pews each Sunday. They must
lead God's children into a place of holiness before
God. Instead of entering into a process of repen-
tance, God's people have been in the process of
justification. They're trying to justify their sin, but
God has a way of making us accountable.

Israel tried to wink at Achan's sin: "Well, he didn't take much, and we don't want to bother Joshua with it. After all, he's had a long, hard week." But look what happened to the children of Israel as a result of Achan's sin:

> *And Joshua sent men from Jericho to Ai, which is beside Bethaven, on the east side of Bethel, and spake unto them, saying, Go up and view the country. And the men went up and viewed Ai. And they returned to Joshua, and said unto him, Let not all the people go up; but let about two or three thousand men go up and smite Ai; and make not all the people to labour thither; for they are but few. So there went up thither of the people about three thousand men: and they fled before the men of Ai. And the men of Ai smote of them about thirty and six men: for they chased them from before the gate even unto Shebarim, and smote them in the going down: wherefore the hearts of the people melted, and became as water.*   Joshua 7:2-5

Not very long after that great victory at Jericho, the Israelites were defeated in battle. Why? Because Achan broke Israel's covenant with God. Today people break their covenants with God all the time. They take their commitments lightly, expecting God to ignore their sins.

We've all known people who get into a tight spot and make all kinds of promises to God — if He will only help them out of their trouble. Then, when the crisis is past, they start vacillating, "Well, God, You know I didn't understand what I was saying. I was under stress. I didn't really mean that." What they end up doing is breaking their covenant with God, a very dangerous thing to do.

Samson had a covenant with God. He was a Nazarite, and that meant that he had vowed never to touch dead carcasses, never to drink alcoholic beverages, and never to cut his hair. When Samson broke that covenant with God, the Philistines captured him, burned out his eyes, and made him tread out grain with the oxen at the grist mill. He lost God's supernatural protection when he broke God's covenant. And when the children of Israel broke their covenant in the Promised Land, they also lost God's protective covering.

When Achan sinned, all of Israel suffered; for Achan's sin was the responsibility of the whole camp. Thirty-six men died in the battle with Ai. That may not sound like very many out of three thousand men, but not one man died in the battle for Jericho. Not a single drop of blood was shed. No one was injured. There wasn't a skinned knee in the whole camp that day.

The name *"Jericho"* means *"a place of fragrance."* Jericho was blooming like a flower; it was a prosperous, innovative, mighty city. Yet Israel took this powerful city without losing a man. On the other hand, the name *"Ai"* means *"the place of ruin."* Obviously, Ai could not be compared with Jericho.

Because of that, the Israelites decided that they could conquer Ai with just a few thousand men. And maybe they could have. But when they went to war with sin in their camp, they were turned to flight.

When we go to war with sin in our camp, we forfeit God's power to work on our behalf. You and I cannot defeat the devil in our own strength. We must realize that our might and power does not lie in our checkbooks or savings accounts. It's not in our education or physical stamina. No! Our ability to change situations and win battles still lies in God and only in God.

In our own strength, we don't even have what it takes to defeat Ai, a heap of ruins. The enemy will drive us back to our little church buildings and say, "You stay there until we say you can come out again." Our enemies will rob us of our children, our finances, our marriages, our careers, and our cities. They will claim everything we own for their own.

When we are in good standing with God and go out to fight in His strength, we have nothing to fear. When we fight on God's terms, the victory is ours but the battle is His.

Israel was defeated at Ai:

> *And Joshua rent his clothes, and fell to the earth upon his face before the ark of the* Lord *until the eventide, he and the elders of Israel, and put dust upon their heads.*   Joshua 7:6

I can picture Joshua lying there on the ground, moaning and groaning, crying and complaining.

Most of us have felt that way before; so despondent that we just throw ourselves on the bed and sob. That's essentially what Joshua did. He threw himself down on the earthen floor and began crying out to God:

> *And Joshua said, Alas, O LORD GOD, wherefore hast thou at all brought this people over Jordan, to deliver us into the hand of the Amorites, to destroy us? would to God we had been content, and dwelt on the other side Jordan! O LORD, what shall I say, when Israel turneth their backs before their enemies! For the Canaanites and all the inhabitants of the land shall hear of it, and shall environ us round, and cut off our name from the earth: and what wilt thou do unto thy great name?*   Joshua 7:7-9

Joshua was afraid that other enemies of Israel would hear about their defeat and would come and wipe them out:

> *And the LORD said unto Joshua, Get thee up; wherefore liest thou thus upon thy face?*
>   Joshua 7:10

God was saying, "Get up off the floor, Joshua. You're not accomplishing anything through your depression. You must deal with the sin in your camp":

> *Israel hath sinned, and they have also transgressed my covenant which I commanded them:*

*for they have even taken of the accursed thing,
and have also stolen, and dissembled also, and
they have put it even among their own stuff.
Therefore the children of Israel could not stand
before their enemies, but turned their backs before their enemies, because they were accursed:
neither will I be with you any more, except ye
destroy the accursed from among you.*

Joshua 7:11-12

God revealed to Joshua who it was who had
sinned. Notice that Joshua didn't catch Achan in his
sin. Caleb didn't catch him. The Levites didn't catch
him. The members of his tribe didn't catch him. But
God knew Achan's sin, and He revealed it to Joshua.
If you think that you're safe with your "secret" sin,
remember that God knows all about your sin and He
won't think twice about revealing it — if He needs
to.

God told Joshua what to do to get the sin out of the
camp:

*So Joshua rose up early in the morning, and
brought Israel by their tribes; and the tribe of
Judah was taken: And he brought the family of
Judah; and he took the family of the Zarhites:
and he brought the family of the Zarhites man by
man; and Zabdi was taken: And he brought his
household man by man; and Achan, the son of
Carmi, the son of Zabdi, the son of Zerah, of the
tribe of Judah, was taken. And Joshua said unto*

Achan, My son, give, I pray thee, glory to the
LORD *God of Israel, and make confession unto*
him; and tell me now what thou hast done; hide
it not from me. And Achan answered Joshua,
and said, Indeed I have sinned against the LORD
God of Israel, and thus and thus have I done:

Joshua 7:16-20

God had already shown Joshua who was at fault
and exactly what he had done. But through this process of elimination, God showed all of Israel that He
knew their sin and that He held the entire nation
accountable. Achan, with his whole family, was
stoned to death and burned because of his disobedi-
ence.

The conclusions are striking. Breaking God's covenants is a serious thing. Our sins not only affect us
personally, but all those around us as well. Our dis-
obedience to God's laws affects our families and the
entire Body of Christ. How we live from day to day
counts. Our words count, and our actions count.
And that is important because we cannot win battles
when we contradict God's plan.

You can be the first hindrance to possession. You
can be your own worst enemy. If you want to be a
conqueror, learn to listen carefully to what the Lord
says to you and be obedient to Him.

Those who are inconsistent in their daily lives
might win one battle, only to fall at Ai. Get sin out of
your camp so that you can continue to move forward
to possess all the land which God has put before you.

Sin in your life is the first hindrance to possession.

Chapter 10

The Second Hindrance to Possession: Kings

And the LORD *said unto Joshua, Fear not, neither be thou dismayed: take all the people of war with thee, and arise, go up to Ai: see, I have given into thy hand the king of Ai, and his people, and his city, and his land:*   Joshua 8:1

God told Joshua to take all of his soldiers to war with him. It had been a mistake not to take everyone against Ai. Having seen how easy it was to take Jericho and seeing how small Ai seemed compared to Jericho, they decided that they didn't need their entire army to win the battle. But God said that when it is time to fight, the whole army must go to war.

Notice here what God promised to give the Israel-ites: *"the king of Ai, and his people, and his city, and his land."*

Why was it so important to capture the king? Because the king symbolized the devil himself, the ruler of the evil stronghold. He was the power behind the people:

> *And it came to pass, when all the kings which were on this side Jordan, in the hills, and in the valleys, and in all the coasts of the great sea over against Lebanon, the Hittite, and the Amorite, the Canaanite, the Perizzite, the Hivite, and the Jebusite, heard thereof; That they gathered themselves together, to fight with Joshua and with Israel, with one accord. And when the inhabitants of Gibeon heard what Joshua had done unto Jericho and to Ai, They did work wilily, and went and made as if they had been ambassadors, and took old sacks upon their asses, and wine bottles, old, and rent, and bound up; And old shoes and clouted upon their feet, and old garments upon them; and all the bread of their provision was dry and mouldy. And they went to Joshua unto the camp at Gilgal, and said unto him, and to the men of Israel, We be come from a far country: now therefore make ye a league with us.*   Joshua 9:1-6

The Gibeonites were some of the evil inhabitants of the land of Canaan. They decided to trick the Israelites into making a covenant with them. They had heard that God told the Israelites to kill all of their enemies and to drive them from the land, and they were afraid for their lives. So they arrived in Joshua's camp one day claiming to be from a great distance:

> *And the men took of their victuals, and asked not counsel at the mouth of the LORD. And Joshua made peace with them, and made a league with them, to let them live: and the princes of the congregation sware unto them.*
>
> Joshua 9:14-15

The Israelites failed to seek God's will in this matter; and Joshua made a pact with the Gibeonites, promising not to kill them. When you and I fail to seek God's will in every matter, we can enter into pacts with the world which may seem intelligent and reasonable but which will end in destruction:

> *And it came to pass at the end of three days after they had made a league with them, that they heard that they were their neighbours, and that they dwelt among them.*   Joshua 9:16

> *And the children of Israel smote them not, because the princes of the congregation had sworn unto them by the LORD God of Israel. And all the congregation murmured against the princes. But all the princes said unto all the congregation, We have sworn unto them by the LORD God*

*of Israel: now therefore we may not touch them.
This we will do to them; we will even let them
live, lest wrath be upon us, because of the oath
which we sware unto them.*   Joshua 9:18-20

*And Joshua made them that day hewers of wood
and drawers of water for the congregation, and
for the altar of the* LORD, *even unto this day, in
the place which he should choose.*

Joshua 9:27

The Israelites realized, too late, that they couldn't
kill the Gibeonites, as the Lord had commanded, because they had made a pact with them. Their
experience with Achan had taught them the conse-
quences of breaking a covenant, and they could not
turn back, although their league with the enemy kept
them from carrying out God's instructions. When
you and I make a deal with the enemy, when we sign
a peace treaty with the devil, it keeps us from obeying God's commands and from receiving God's
rewards.

We must not vacillate between following God and
following the world. We must carry out God's orders
to the letter, or we may find ourselves in a situation
which will wreak havoc on our lives.

When we follow God, no enemy can stand against
us. At one point, five kings decided to join forces
against the Israelites because they had heard the reports that God's people were conquering the land.
The devil thinks he can win if he gangs up on you.
But look what happened to those five kings:

And there was no day like that before it or after it, that the LORD *hearkened unto the voice of a man: for the* LORD *fought for Israel.*

Joshua 10:14

But these five kings fled, and hid themselves in a cave at Makkedah. Joshua 10:16

Then said Joshua, Open the mouth of the cave, and bring out those five kings unto me out of the cave. Joshua 10:22

And it came to pass, when they brought out those kings unto Joshua, that Joshua called for all the men of Israel, and said unto the captains of the men of war which went with him, Come near, put your feet upon the necks of these kings. And they came near, and put their feet upon the necks of them. And Joshua said unto them, Fear not, nor be dismayed, be strong and of good courage: for thus shall the LORD *do to all your enemies against whom ye fight.*

Joshua 10:24-25

Joshua was exhorting his men to be courageous because the Lord was on their side. God has always fought for His people.

God spoke to the prophet Jeremiah about facing evil kingdoms:

Be not afraid of their faces: for I am with thee to deliver thee, saith the LORD. Jeremiah 1:8

See, I have this day set thee over the nations and over the kingdoms, to root out, and to pull down, and to destroy, and to throw down, to build, and to plant.   Jeremiah 1:10

Notice that instead of doing it himself, Joshua called his men to stand on the necks of these kings. He was illustrating to his people that they, too, had the power through God to put the enemy under their feet. You have power through Jesus. He said that He has given us *power to tread on serpents and scorpions, and over all the power of the enemy.*

Joshua was saying to his men, "Just let them know that with a twist of your foot you can crush their voice box. Let them know that you have authority over them. Go ahead. Put your feet on their necks." Before it was over, thirty-one kings had fallen to the Israelites (see Joshua 12:24).

That is what God had promised. He said: *"I have given into thy hand the king of Ai, and his people, and his city, and his land."* The taking of the king is always key to taking the people and the land. When the king falls, the people and the land become vulnerable. If you want to rescue your children, your friends, your loved ones, your neighbors, your cities, and your nation from the grip of the enemy, then you must first "kill the king" that is controlling them.

David showed us that our warfare is not carnal, but spiritual:

Let the high praises of God be in their mouth, and a two-edged sword in their hand; To execute

> *vengeance upon the heathen, and punishments upon the people; To bind their kings with chains, and their nobles with fetters of iron; To execute upon them the judgment written: this honour have all his saints. Praise ye the LORD.*
>
> Psalms 149:6-9

This is not a battle against personalities. It is against those *"principalities,"* against that *"spiritual wickedness in high places."*

Daniel prayed and fasted for twenty-one days, seeking God's wisdom for the children of Israel because of their long captivity. He knew that it was time for them to be set free. The enemy of their souls, however, sought to hinder that prayer; and the angel whom God had dispatched with His answer to Daniel's prayer was held up by the prince of the kingdom of Persia. Eventually, Michael, one of God's chief princes, joined forces with the angel to defeat the kings of Persia and the victory was won. That was a spiritual battle, and Daniel fought it on his knees in prayer.

Moses had to combat Pharaoh for the release of the Israelites from Egypt. His confrontation with Pharaoh symbolizes our own battle with the spiritual kings that are controlling people, cities, and nations today. You and I must seek God through prayer and fasting and defeat spiritual kings with the sword of the Spirit. We must enter into spiritual warfare to "kill those kings" and to release our friends and loved ones from their evil grip.

Joshua had no respect or mercy for the thirty-one kings he conquered. First, he utterly humiliated them; then he killed them. Christians today seem to have too much respect for the devil, almost as if they are afraid to violate his civil rights. We must be willing to destroy every spiritual king who has tried to build strongholds in our lives—strongholds of jealousy, immorality, depression, and temper tantrums. Put them under your feet, once and for all. Show no mercy. Utterly destroy them.

You may feel that you can't do it. But you can — through faith in Jesus Christ. It is true that you can't do it in the flesh, but you can do it in the Spirit:

> *Are ye so foolish? having begun in the Spirit,*
> *are ye now made perfect by the flesh?*
> Galatians 3:3

When you became born again, you did it through faith in Jesus Christ, not through the works of your flesh. You cannot be saved by the works of the flesh. Neither can you be made perfect by your flesh. Being perfected requires faith in God. And we get that faith by hearing and reading God's Word:

> *So then faith cometh by hearing, and hearing by*
> *the word of God.*   Romans 10:17

Immediately following the Israelites' victory at Ai, Joshua took time out to read God's law to his people; and they willingly stood and listened:

*And afterward he read all the words of the law,
the blessings and cursings, according to all that
is written in the book of the law. There was not a
word of all that Moses commanded, which
Joshua read not before all the congregation of
Israel, with the women, and the little ones, and
the strangers that were conversant among them.*
                                        Joshua 8:34-35

Imagine how long it must have taken to read Genesis, Exodus, Leviticus, Numbers, and Deuteronomy. Yet the people stood and listened to the reading of *"all the words of the law,"* even the women and children.

Joshua recognized the importance of keeping the Word of God sown into our hearts, even when we have just experienced a great victory. It may be even more important at that moment because human nature has a tendency to relax when things are going well, and God's people are no different in this regard. When we have won a great personal victory or a great victory for God's Kingdom, we often get lax and don't pray as much as we did when we were in the heat of the battle. We don't fast as much as we did when we were intent on fighting a known enemy. We quit listening to the voice of the Holy Spirit; we let down our guard; and the devil seizes that moment to come in the back door and attack us. This is one of the reasons we win at Jericho and lose at Ai.

Elijah had called fire down from heaven—fire which burned up the sacrifice, the wood, the stones, the dust, and even licked up the water in the trench around the altar. He had prayed for rain and it came. He had outrun Ahab's horses to the entrance of Jezreel. But after he had experienced these incredible miracles, he let down his guard:

> *And Ahab told Jezebel all that Elijah had done, and withal how he had slain all the prophets with the sword. Then Jezebel sent a messenger unto Elijah, saying, So let the gods do to me, and more also, if I make not thy life as the life of one of them by to morrow about this time. And when he saw that, he arose, and went for his life, and came to Beersheba, which belongeth to Judah, and left his servant there. But he himself went a day's journey into the wilderness, and came and sat down under a juniper tree: and he requested for himself that he might die; and said, it is enough; now, O LORD, take away my life; for I am not better than my fathers.*
>
> 1 Kings 19:1-4

Jezebel, the pagan wife of King Ahab, sent a message to Elijah that she was going to have him killed; and he was frightened by it and ran for his life. Eventually, he crawled under a juniper tree and begged God to let him die. What had changed? God's ability to work miracles for Elijah was still the same. God's desire for Elijah to be victorious in every situation was still the same. Only Elijah had changed. He had become lax after his previous victories and had allowed the devil to put fear in his heart.

Clearly, God does not want us to fear any enemy:

> *For God hath not given us the spirit of fear; but of power, and of love, and of a sound mind.*
> 2 Timothy 1:7

God had said to Joshua:

> *Fear not, neither be thou dismayed: take all the people of war with thee, and arise, go up to Ai: see, I have given into thy hand the king of Ai, and his people, and his city, and his land:*
> Joshua 8:1

Joshua wasn't commanded to trust in his soldiers. They could not deliver Ai into his hand. He was not told to put his confidence in the priests and Levites. They could not overcome such strong enemies. He was encouraged to trust God because He is greater than any enemy and all enemies. And because Joshua trusted God, he was not to be afraid. The battle is the Lord's.

Why is it that every time we win a battle, we tend to think that we just "got lucky"? We are almost surprised when we win. But we are not destined for defeat; we are destined for victory. We are not destined to live under the yoke of the devil; we are destined to break his hold. We must be thankful for every victory; and at the same time, we must realize that winning is part of our inheritance. God did not intend for us to be poverty-stricken, disease-ridden, or mentally inept. He did not intend for us to be confused, depressed, or downtrodden. He created us to rise up in the power of the Holy Ghost and put the devil under our feet. He wants us to be people of continuing conquests.

Jesus said:

> *And from the days of John the Baptist until now the kingdom of heaven suffereth violence, and the violent take it by force.*   Matthew 11:12

The devil isn't passive; he is violent. And we have to get violent, too, in order to defeat him.

The Apostle Peter exhorts us to:

> *Be sober, be vigilant; because your adversary the devil, as a roaring lion, walketh about, seeking whom he may devour:*   1 Peter 5:8

James, in his letter to the churches, tells us how to make the enemy flee:

> *Submit yourselves therefore to God. Resist the devil, and he will flee from you.*   James 4:7

When you are submitted to God, you have all the power of the Holy Ghost backing you up. You cannot fail to conquer the enemy.

The devil acts like a lion, yet Christians have the authority to send him running with his tail between his legs. To us, he is "all bark and no bite." He's not really a lion. He just acts like one. He has nothing on us because God gives us the boldness of a lion as well:

> *The wicked flee when no man pursueth: but the*
> *righteous are bold as a lion.*   Proverbs 28:1

You and I are to possess our Promised Land with violence; we are to rise up with a mighty roar against the enemy!

> *The* LORD *shall go forth as a mighty man, he*
> *shall stir up jealousy like a man of war: he shall*
> *cry, yea, roar; he shall prevail against his en-*
> *emies. I have long time holden my peace; I have*
> *been still, and refrained myself: now will I cry*
> *like a travailing woman; I will destroy and de-*
> *vour at once.*   Isaiah 42:13-14

It doesn't say that God will whisper. No! He will roar against His enemies! So don't hold back any longer. Now is the time for us to utterly destroy the enemy. Now is the time for us to kill the evil kings and to continue our conquest of all that God has prepared for us. What are we waiting for?

In a very short time, by taking the evil kings one at a time, God's people had gained a foothold in the land and knew their place of authority. If we could only realize God's great purpose for each of our lives, we would also take hold of the authority God has placed in our hands as believers:

> *For as many as are led by the Spirit of God, they are the sons of God. For ye have not received the spirit of bondage again to fear; but ye have received the Spirit of adoption, whereby we cry, Abba, Father. The Spirit itself beareth witness with our spirit, that we are the children of God: And if children, then heirs; heirs of God, and joint-heirs with Christ; if so be that we suffer with him, that we may be also glorified together.*
> Romans 8:14-17

We have authority on this earth as the children of Almighty God. We are determined to drive out every pagan king and to take back what is rightfully ours. Look out, Devil, we are moving into our Promised Land to possess our prophetic promises.

Chapter 11

Taking Possession

*Now Joshua was old and stricken in years; and
the* LORD *said unto him, Thou art old and
stricken in years, and there remaineth yet very
much land to be possessed.* Joshua 13:1

Just as Joshua's victories gave the people of God a
firm footing in the Promised Land, Jesus' victory on
the cross two thousand years ago firmly established
us as Christians in the Kingdom of God. And just as
Joshua killed the thirty-one kings and took back their
territory which God had destined for His people,
Jesus spoiled principalities and established our secure future. We are now joint heirs with Him.

But that doesn't mean that we can relax or that everything is accomplished for us. When Joshua came to the end of his days on earth, he had to say, *"There remaineth yet very much land to be possessed."* Not everything promised to God's people prophetically had been possessed. Because Joshua is a type of Christ, this has a strong spiritual application for Christians today.

Jesus didn't completely build the Kingdom of God before He went away. He told His disciples:

> *Nevertheless I tell you the truth; It is expedient for you that I go away: for if I go not away, the Comforter will not come unto you; but if I depart, I will send him unto you.* John 16:7

Joshua's passing was prophetic, looking to the coming life of Christ. He didn't do it all for his people. He got them started; then he left territory for them to possess themselves. And Jesus did the same for us.

Both Moses and Joshua had been given instructions from the Lord on how to divide up the Promised Land, what area to ascribe to what tribe of Israel. The land was divided into sections, much like every country is divided into states or provinces. Each tribe was assigned an area and inherited the cities and the resources contained in that territory. But if there were heathen kings and tribes still living in those areas ascribed to them, each tribe had to fight to take what was theirs.

It is important to notice that they didn't choose for themselves the plot of land they wanted. That would have resulted in chaos. God divided the land for them; He knows what is best for each of us. He divided the land according to the size of each tribe. For example, Benjamin was a small tribe and didn't need as much land as the tribe of Judah did. So, if all the land had been divided up equally, Benjamin wouldn't have had enough people to occupy and guard all of its territory and Judah would have been too crowded. God gave each tribe exactly what it needed to survive. Trust God, for He always knows best.

Some of God's people today are trying to possess everything they lay their eyes on. And that is not God's plan. He has set definite boundaries around our territories. He has already decided the terms of our inheritance. Why some Christians always think that the grass is greener on the other side of the fence I don't know. They are always trying to possess more than their share. God hasn't promised to give you everything your eyes lust after. He has promised to give you the desires of a pure heart.

Learn to trust God's judgment. If He says that something is part of your inheritance, then you may rise up in faith and possess it. But if God hasn't given it to you, don't waste your time and His resources trying to possess it. Leave it alone.

When the children of Israel were in the desert, they decided they wanted meat to eat. Oh, how they wanted meat! They were no longer satisfied with God's menu of manna from heaven. They just had to have meat. They murmured and complained so much about it that finally God changed the menu and gave them the flesh they had been seeking. Then they ate quail until they were sick of quail, and they died with the flesh *"yet between their teeth"* (Numbers 11:33).

Too many Christians today want the things of the flesh; and like the Israelites in the wilderness, they complain so much that God finally allows them to have what they want. When they get it, they find that it is not the Bread of Life that God has prepared for them and they die with the flesh *"yet between their teeth."* This is a tragedy that ought not to be. The lust of the flesh is a form of rebellion against God and always results in death.

Rebelling against God, wanting something that is not His will for your life, is a very dangerous thing; and God's people should know better. Yet the Israelites rebelled even as they were possessing their Promised Land:

> *Yet the children of Manasseh could not drive out the inhabitants of those cities; but the Canaanites would dwell in that land. Yet it came to pass, when the children of Israel were waxen strong, that they put the Canaanites to tribute, but did not utterly drive them out.*
>
> Joshua 17:12-13

God told the children of Israel to obliterate the Canaanites, but someone decided that they had a better idea. They would take advantage of the pagans as a source of revenue. They would allow them to remain in the land but make them pay taxes. "What a great idea!" I can hear someone saying. Wrong! It is never a good idea to compromise with the world and never a good idea to disobey the Lord's express commands. The failure to drive out the Canaanites resulted in other problems:

> *And the children of Joseph spake unto Joshua, saying, Why hast thou given me but one lot and one portion to inherit, seeing I am a great people, forasmuch as the* LORD *hath blessed me hitherto?*
> Joshua 17:14

The descendants of Joseph were complaining about the size of the territory they had been given. It didn't seem to them to be large enough to sustain their farms and houses. But if they had obeyed God and driven out the Canaanites, they would have had plenty of space. They didn't have it because they hadn't obeyed God and given their enemies the eviction notice.

If you are guilty of complaining about the size of the inheritance you are given — in ministry, in relationships, in health, in peaceful households, in jobs — know that your plight is not God's fault. If you are cramped, perhaps it is because you have failed to drive out the enemy that is living on your land.

Joshua had the right answer:

> *And Joshua answered them, If thou be a great*
> *people, then get thee up to the wood country,*
> *and cut down for thyself there in the land of the*
> *Perizzites and of the giants, if mount Ephraim*
> *be too narrow for thee.*   Joshua 17:15

If your place is too small, take more territory. You
haven't possessed it all yet. *"There remaineth yet very*
much land to be possessed." Don't wait around for others to do your work for you. You must dispossess
your enemies and possess your territory. Don't expect to have it handed to you on a silver platter:

> *And the children of Joseph said, The hill is not*
> *enough for us: and all the Canaanites that dwell*
> *in the land of the valley have chariots of iron,*
> *both they who are of Bethshean and her towns,*
> *and they who are of the valley of Jezreel.*
>   Joshua 17:16

The enemy always looks formidable. These had
"chariots of iron." Could the tribe of Joseph conquer
such a mighty force? Were the Israelites returning to
the grasshopper mentality that they had left on the
other side of the Jordan? Why does it always seem
easier to cohabit with devils than to drive them out?

Too many Christians today find it easier to cohabit
and put up with people who are bound by the devil
than to take their authority over those spirits. *It's*

easier to join them than to fight them, they think. But they're soon going to be jolted awake by the realization that the people of God simply cannot dwell peacefully with the devil. Eventually, there will be war.

For a while, there was an unusual peace:

> *And the land had rest from war.*
> Joshua 14:15

What a wonderful thought! Peace! Rest from war! But this was a false peace. There can be no peace when there are heathen in our land. This was no peace; it was only a temporary respite. It may have seemed easier to get the Canaanites to pay taxes than to fight them, but cohabiting with the devil will never end in peace.

People have said to me: "You know, it seems like as soon as I made up my mind to fight this sickness, or this poverty, then all hell broke loose." Of course it did. As soon as you make up your mind to fight, you are immediately engaged in a spiritual battle. You are fighting with spirits of disease or spirits of poverty. And don't expect the devil to be happy about that. You are tearing down his kingdom, and he can't take that sitting down. Don't expect him to leave you alone. If you are going to possess your prophetic promise, you must fight for it.

Many are tired of the battle and have decided that they want to take a vacation from war. But let me warn you: the devil never takes a vacation from this war, and neither can you. You must fight until you have total victory. You must fight until the war is finished. And it is not finished until your enemy is totally destroyed:

> *And Joshua spake unto the house of Joseph, even to Ephraim and to Manasseh, saying, Thou art a great people, and hast great power: thou shalt not have one lot only: But the mountain shall be thine; for it is a wood, and thou shalt cut it down: and the outgoings of it shall be thine: for thou shalt drive out the Canaanites, though they have iron chariots, and though they be strong.*
> Joshua 17:17-18

These people were capable of taking their own territory. They just needed motivation. They just needed encouragement. It didn't matter how many iron chariots the enemy had. These were God's people. "You can do it," Joshua was saying.

There are many people in the Church today who have come so far, only to fail to possess. They have crossed the Jordan, destroyed Jericho, defeated Ai, killed some kings, and have a strong foothold in the land. But there are still some devils trespassing on their property, and they seem unwilling or unable to do anything about it. They are so near, and yet so far from total possession.

A great majority of the Christians I know would fit into that category. They know that they are children of God. They know that God has power. They know what their inheritance is. But for some reason, they haven't yet possessed what is theirs. They seem to be looking down at the fertile valley saying, "Just look at all those iron chariots. Look at those devils trampling our fertile, green countryside. Look at those heathen exalting themselves against the knowledge of God."

We seem to be experts on knowing and describing the problem, yet powerless to do anything about it. Rise up, Church, and drive those devils out of the land.

We pray and cry and plead, asking God for miracles. And God is waiting for us to rise up and possess. Don't misunderstand me. Prayer is not bad. It takes prayer and fasting to maintain the power of God in our lives. But prayer and fasting is not enough; and sometimes it is time to stop praying and time to start chasing devils.

We have been putting off the natural man and putting on the spiritual man long enough. It is time to use that spiritual man and move in possession.

If someone slaps your face, your natural man says to rip him limb from limb. The supernatural man, however, says to turn the other cheek.

If your brother needs a coat, your natural man tells him to go out and get his own coat. The supernatural man, however, gives him your coat and your overcoat too.

If you get into a financial bind, your natural man says to keep your tithes and offerings until you get through the problem. The supernatural man, however, says to sow bountifully with the assurance that you will reap bountifully.

If you become sick or tired, your natural man says to stay home from church and rest from doing God's work. The supernatural man, however, says, *"Let God arise and His enemies be scattered."*

If you become depressed, your natural man wants to curl up in the corner and have a "pity party." But the supernatural man says, *"The joy of the* LORD *is your strength."*

It is not easy to walk in the supernatural. That is only part of the battle. But realize that if you are to win, you must walk in the supernatural. If you are to evict the enemy from your land, if you are to rise up and possess your inheritance, then you cannot rest from the battle.

Drive out those unclean spirits that are hindering your divine health. Drive out those demons that are hindering your prosperity. Give no mercy to the enemies who are tormenting your children. Rise up and say:

> "Satan, Jesus has given me the keys to healing and divine health. He has given me the keys to prosperity and financial success. He has given me the keys to raising godly children and maintaining a strong marriage. Stand aside because I am taking back what belongs to me. I am possessing my Promised Land!"

The people of Joshua's day had to do the same:

> *And the whole congregation of the children of*
> *Israel assembled together at Shiloh, and set up*
> *the tabernacle of the congregation there. And the*
> *land was subdued before them.*   Joshua 18:1

Other nations were still inhabiting the land, but
they were no longer attacking the children of Israel.
They were subdued — for the moment. That didn't
change the fact that God had told His people to rid
the land of the evil inhabitants, not to subdue them:

> *And there remained among the children of Israel*
> *seven tribes, which had not yet received their*
> *inheritance. And Joshua said unto the children*
> *of Israel, How long are ye slack to go to possess*
> *the land, which the* LORD *God of your fathers*
> *hath given you?*   Joshua 18:2-3

To Joshua, not possessing was being *"slack."* What
was wrong with these people? They had come so far,
yet they had still not possessed. I hear God saying to
the Church today, "How long will you remain slack
in possessing what is yours?"

Joshua was determined to get these people
moving:

> *Give out from among you three men for each*
> *tribe: and I will send them, and they shall rise,*
> *and go through the land, and describe it accord-*

> *ing to the inheritance of them; and they shall*
> *come again to me.*   Joshua 18:4

He wanted them to see what they were missing and come back and tell everyone else about it. That's why some men and women of God today sound to us as if they have seen something the rest of us haven't seen yet. God has let them walk on their land so that they could tell the rest of us what we are missing.

Rise up, Church, and go forth! Issue an eviction notice to every enemy, and don't rest until you have taken all that is rightfully yours.

Chapter 12

The Priests and Possession

Then came near the heads of the fathers of the Levites unto Eleazar the priest, and unto Joshua the son of Nun, and unto the heads of the fathers of the tribes of the children of Israel; And they spake unto them at Shiloh in the land of Canaan, saying, The LORD *commanded by the hand of Moses to give us cities to dwell in, with the suburbs thereof for our cattle.*   Joshua 21:1-2

This is a very interesting passage. *"The heads of the fathers of the Levites"* called a meeting, and it wasn't just to have tea and cookies. They came together to render a judgment. The Levites were the priestly tribe, and they came together this day to consider the question of their inheritance.

When the Promised Land was divided among the various tribes, the Levites were not included. The Lord had not given them any land:

> *But unto the Levites he gave none inheritance among them.*   Joshua 14:3

> *And the* LORD *spake unto Aaron, Thou shalt have no inheritance in their land, neither shalt thou have any part among them: I am thy part and thine inheritance among the children of Israel. And, behold, I have given the children of Levi all the tenth in Israel for an inheritance, for their service which they serve, even the service of the tabernacle of the congregation. Neither must the children of Israel henceforth come nigh the tabernacle of the congregation, lest they bear sin, and die. But the Levites shall do the service of the tabernacle of the congregation, and they shall bear their iniquity: it shall be a statute for ever throughout your generations, that among the children of Israel they have no inheritance. But the tithes of the children of Israel, which they offer as an heave offering unto the* LORD, *I have given to the Levites to inherit: therefore I have said unto them, Among the children of Israel they shall have no inheritance.*
> Numbers 18:20-24

The Levites were to be supported by the tithe from the other tribes. Also, each tribe was to provide a certain number of cities in which the Levites could live. They would have full use of the surrounding fields for farming and pasture land. In this way, the Levites could dedicate themselves to the service of the Lord — whether they liked it or not.

Paul said:

> *For the gifts and calling of God are without re-*
> *pentance.* Romans 11:29

The Levites had no choice but to work in the ministry. They couldn't say, "I'm tired of this job. My boss hassles me, and I'm grossly underpaid. I think I'll quit and look for another job." They didn't have that luxury; for they were called to oversee the spiritual life of the nation. Because of that, possessing land would be a distraction for them, taking their time away from more important things. They were to live by faith in God.

The Levites were not, however, beggars. They, too, had their Promised Land. Keeping God's servants poor and broke is not scriptural. Since the other tribes gave a tenth of their increase to the Levites, the Levites were able to possess as much as anyone else in Israel.

Many people believe that ministers must be poor in order to maintain their spirituality. That is not true. If it were, we would all have to be poor to qualify for heaven. Ministers should receive their just reward and should be able to raise their families without fear of financial failure. To ensure that this is the case, all of God's people must be faithful with their tithes and offerings for those who are dedicated to spiritual service.

Paul wrote to the church at Corinth:

> *Am I not free? Am I not an apostle? Have I not seen Jesus our Lord? Are you not the result of my work in the Lord? Even though I may not be an apostle to others, surely I am to you! For you are the seal of my apostleship in the Lord. This is my defense to those who sit in judgment on me. Don't we have the right to food and drink? Don't we have the right to take a believing wife along with us, as do the other apostles and the Lord's brothers and Cephas? Or is it only I and Barnabas who must work for a living?*
> 1 Corinthians 9:1-6/NIV

Paul and Barnabas were forced to find secular employment and go to work because the Corinthian Christians were not fulfilling their responsibility to support the ministry. This is clearly not correct:

> *Who serves as a soldier at his own expense? Who plants a vineyard and does not eat of its grapes? Who tends a flock and does not drink of the milk?* 1 Corinthians 9:7/NIV

How many people do you know who draw from their own savings accounts in order to serve in the

Army, Navy, Air Force, or Marines? And who works a field without hope of harvesting a material blessing? And who tends a flock without the expectation of receiving just pay?

Paul continued:

> *Do I say this merely from a human point of view? Doesn't the Law say the same thing? For it is written in the Law of Moses: "Do not muzzle an ox while it is treading out the grain." Is it about oxen that God is concerned? Surely he says this for us, doesn't he? Yes, this was written for us, because when the plowman plows and the thresher threshes, they ought to do so in the hope of sharing in the harvest. If we have sown spiritual seed among you, is it too much if we reap a material harvest from you?*
>
> 1 Corinthians 9:8-11/NIV

We cannot afford to be selfish where our spiritual leaders are concerned. They may not be plowing and sowing and reaping in the natural sense, but they are doing all that and more in the spiritual realm. Therefore, they should not be muzzled. They should be allowed to partake of the blessing. They sow to us the spiritual things, and they have a right to reap our material things in exchange:

> *If others have this right of support from you, shouldn't we have it all the more? But we did not use this right. On the contrary, we put up*

> *with anything rather than hinder the gospel of Christ. Don't you know that those who work in the temple get their food from the temple, and those who serve at the altar share in what is offered on the altar?*
>
>   1 Corinthians 9:12-13/NIV

Ministers have suffered far too much in this regard, kept poor so that they could be controlled. They have been put through unbelievable circumstances for the sake of the Gospel, when, clearly, they have as much right to financial blessing as the Christian Realtor or the Christian CPA or the Christian attorney:

> *In the same way, the Lord has commanded that those who preach the gospel should receive their living from the gospel.*
>
>   1 Corinthians 9:14/NIV

The Levites did not starve to death or need to beg to provide for their families. They received a tenth from each tribe, enough for them to live comfortably. They lived from the ministry. And today ministers who dedicate their entire lives to God and His people should be blessed with the tithe of the land. They don't deserve to be forced to live in poverty or to have people look at them in disrespect because they are less than someone else.

Some think that the proper income might be a distraction to ministers and cause them to stop serving

God. If that is true, we should never pay soldiers either.

The Bible says:

> *Endure hardship with us like a good soldier of Christ Jesus. No one serving as a soldier gets involved in civilian affairs - he wants to please his commanding officer.*
>
> 2 Timothy 2:3-4/NIV

"Enduring hardship" does not mean living in poverty, having no home, and not being able to pay the bills. It simply means *not becoming entangled with material things*. It means that ministers of the Gospel, like all soldiers of Christ, may have material things as long as material things don't have them.

I know a pastor who founded a church with just a few members. For many years he struggled, paying the church bills and supporting his family from the small tithe of the church. He barely survived at times. But he was faithful; God worked for him; and the church grew. It grew until, finally, it had several thousand members.

By this time, the tithes of the church were so substantial that the pastor felt embarrassed and asked the board to put him on a salary. He didn't need that much money to live. They refused. "If you want to give it back to the church, that's your business; but we don't want to make you a hireling," was the answer of those people who had seen his sacrifice of many years to build the congregation.

It is possible to receive God's blessings, to possess your Promised Land, and not become a crook in the process. And there are many good ministers who have done it. There are also many good members who refuse to muzzle their spiritual leaders.

When the special meeting of *"the fathers of the Levites"* was called, Eleazar the priest came with the urim and the thummim. These were two stones which were kept in the front pocket of the ephod which the priest wore and were used to make crucial decisions. Apparently, God would cause one stone to light up when His answer to the Israelites' question was *yes* and the other would light up when God's answer was *no*.

These men were serious about this matter. They were dedicated to their work but felt that they deserved to be properly rewarded. They didn't hold the meeting in secret or sneak around behind the backs of their members. They were proud to stand and say, "God has destined an inheritance for us also. He does not want us to beg for a living or to be forced to take secular work to support our families. It is time for us to take possession of our inheritance."

And the children of Israel responded favorably:

> *And the children of Israel gave unto the Levites out of their inheritance, at the commandment of the* Lord, *these cities and their suburbs.*
>
> Joshua 21:3

> *All the cities of the Levites within the possession*
> *of the children of Israel were forty and eight cit-*
> *ies with their suburbs.* Joshua 21:41

Israel obeyed God and gave to her ministers what God had commanded them to have. In doing so, she lost nothing because that allowed the Levites to concentrate on the spiritual welfare of the entire nation; and the entire nation could prosper under God, as a result. Don't begrudge your spiritual leaders their God-given Promised Land. Do what is required of you to make it possible, and God will always be faithful to bless and prosper you:

> *And the* LORD *gave unto Israel all the land*
> *which he sware to give unto their fathers; and*
> *they possessed it, and dwelt therein. And the*
> LORD *gave them rest round about, according to*
> *all that he sware unto their fathers: and there*
> *stood not a man of all their enemies before them;*
> *the* LORD *delivered all their enemies into their*
> *hand. There failed not ought of any good thing*
> *which the* LORD *had spoken unto the house of*
> *Israel; all came to pass.* Joshua 21:43-45

When the children of Israel became obedient and gave the Levites their just reward, they received all of the blessings which God had promised them.

Giving, as God's Word directs to give, is an act of obedience that helps secure our rightful inheritance in the Lord. Obey God in your giving, and rise up to possess your prophetic promises.

Chapter 13

Challenging Others to Possession

And Joshua gathered all the tribes of Israel to Shechem, and called for the elders of Israel, and for their heads, and for their judges, and for their officers; and they presented themselves before God.   Joshua 24:1

Joshua called together all the key leaders of Israel because he knew that he would soon be passing on his mantle of authority as Israel's leader. He wanted to encourage the people concerning the future and challenge them to possession:

And Joshua said unto all the people, Thus saith the LORD *God of Israel, Your fathers dwelt on the other side of the flood in old time, even Terah, the father of Abraham, and the father of Nachor: and they served other gods. And I took your father Abraham from the other side of the flood, and led him throughout all the land of Canaan, and multiplied his seed, and gave him Isaac.*   Joshua 24:2-3

The next ten verses in Joshua give a brief history of the nation of Israel and recount God's miracles of the past, as Joshua leads the Israelites in thanksgiving for what God has done. This is a very biblical thing to do:

Let us come before his presence with thanksgiving, and make a joyful noise unto him with psalms.   Psalms 95:2

Enter into his gates with thanksgiving, and into his courts with praise: be thankful unto him, and bless his name.   Psalms 100:4

Joshua knew that if the people were to receive his challenge for their future, then they must open their hearts to God.

Now therefore fear the LORD, *and serve him in sincerity and in truth: and put away the gods which your fathers served on the other side of the flood, and in Egypt; and serve ye the LORD. And if it seem evil unto you to serve the LORD, choose you this day whom ye will serve; whether the gods which your fathers served that were on the other side of the flood, or the gods of the Amorites, in whose land ye dwell: but as for me and my house, we will serve the LORD.*

Joshua 24:14-15

Now, you may be thinking, *Nobody has the power to make his family serve God.* But Joshua knew the power of Jehovah God. His God could do anything but fail! And Joshua spoke prophetically and declared that his family would serve the Lord. You see, the spoken Word of God is creative; and when you stand upon God's promises and declare them to be true, they will come to pass in your life.

Solomon said in his proverbs:

Train up a child in the way he should go: and when he is old, he will not depart from it.

Proverbs 22:6

If you want your family to serve God, you find promises in His Word which pertain to your situation and you stand on them. Our Promised Land includes blessings for more than ourselves. We must unite in battle to save our families, our friends, our cities, and our nations.

The tribes of Reuben and Gad and the half tribe of Manasseh found their Promised Land on the east side of the Jordan River. But they didn't forsake their brothers. When it was necessary to go to war against any enemy, the men of those tribes joined the effort. They helped their brothers to drive the enemies from their land and to possess what God had given them. Our possession must not be selfish. We are crossing over into greater things, not just for ourselves, but also for the sake of our brothers and sisters in the Lord. United we will stand against the enemy.

This message is not just for the ladies. Just because the Church is called *the Bride of Christ* doesn't mean that it should consist solely of women. No! Men, take a stand before God and declare His blessings upon your households.

Too many men these days believe that it's *macho* to send their wives and daughters to church while they stay home with their sons drinking beer and watching football on television. But *machismo* will not keep your family out of hell. It will not keep your kids off dope or your daughters from getting pregnant out of wedlock. When trouble came to Israel, Joshua was not too *macho* to fall on his face and call on the name of the Lord. He was not too *macho* to weep before God for the sake of his people.

To be a real man, the man God created you to be, you must be big enough to pray with your family, to set a godly example, to be faithful to go to church, and to pay your tithes. You must teach your children that the only way to live in honesty and integrity is through the strength of the Lord. This is the kind of man Joshua was. We need another generation just like him. His stand moved the people of Israel:

> *And the people answered and said, God forbid that we should forsake the LORD, to serve other gods; For the LORD our God, he it is that brought us up and our fathers out of the land of Egypt, from the house of bondage, and which did those great signs in our sight, and preserved us in all the way wherein we went, and among all the people through whom we passed: And the LORD drave out from before us all the people, even the Amorites which dwelt in the land: therefore will we also serve the LORD; for he is our God. And Joshua said unto the people, Ye cannot serve the LORD: for he is an holy God; he is a jealous God; he will not forgive your transgressions nor your sins. If ye forsake the LORD, and serve strange gods, then he will turn and do you hurt, and consume you, after that he hath done you good. And the people said unto Joshua, Nay; but we will serve the LORD. And Joshua said unto the people, Ye are witnesses against yourselves that ye have chosen you the LORD, to serve him. And they said, We are witnesses.* Joshua 24:16-22*

The children of Israel made a covenant with God, promising not to serve other gods. Each one served as a witness against the other if they should ever break their pledge.

Joshua took this opportunity to exhort his people further:

> *Now therefore put away, said he, the strange gods which are among you, and incline your heart unto the* LORD *God of Israel. And the people said unto Joshua, The* LORD *our God will we serve, and his voice will we obey. So Joshua made a covenant with the people that day, and set them a statute and an ordinance in Shechem. And Joshua wrote these words in the book of the law of God, and took a great stone, and set it up there under an oak, that was by the sanctuary of the* LORD. *And Joshua said unto all the people, Behold, this stone shall be a witness unto us; for it hath heard all the words of the* LORD *which he spake unto us: it shall be therefore a witness unto you, lest ye deny your God. So Joshua let the people depart, every man unto his inheritance. And it came to pass after these things, that Joshua the son of Nun, the servant of the* LORD, *died, being an hundred and ten years old. And they buried him in the border of his inheritance in Timnathserah, which is in mount Ephraim, on the north side of the hill of Gaash. And Israel served the* LORD *all the days of Joshua, and all the days of the elders that overlived Joshua, and which had known all the works of the* LORD, *that he had done for Israel.*   Joshua 24:23-31

One man, by his remembrance of the goodness of God and his desire to love and serve Him, influenced an entire nation to such a degree that everyone was determined to serve God. Joshua realized that he was responsible for much more than his immediate family. His responsibility extended to the great family of Israel. What a man! In good times or bad, he never compromised his stand for God.

What about you? Have you taken a stand for the Lord? Do your coworkers know that you love Jesus? Do your children understand your faith? It may not be the popular thing to do, but it is the right thing to do. And when you take a stand for your faith and refuse to back down, your influence will outlive your physical life span.

This is your reason for living. Will you be one of those who dare to challenge others to possession?

Chapter 14

Now Is the Time

What shall we then say to these things? If God be for us, who can be against us?

Romans 8:31

Now is the time. This is the generation that must rise up in God as never before. More than any other previous generation, we have a greater revelation of who we are and what we have as children of God. God has graciously visited us and has given us prophetic promises.

Aren't you tired of eating manna? Aren't you ready to leave behind the "maintenance mentality"?

It is time to take the land. Are you ready to possess the great things God has promised you?

The terms of our inheritance, our Promised Land, are laid out both in the Bible and in prophetic utterance. God's Word contains the boundaries of our property as well as the rich benefits which are our rights through Jesus Christ.

It is clear that God wants us to have health, prosperity, and blessings. Our inheritance in Him contains happiness, relationship victories, and successful business. Our possessions in Him include strength, joy, peaceful homes, and strong marriages. He doesn't want us to be the victims of every circumstance that comes our way. He wants us to run through troops, leap over walls, and be victorious in every situation.

God is not stingy with His people. He wants to give us hundredfold miracles. He wants to open up the windows of heaven and pour out so many blessings upon us that there will be no room to contain them all. We have all these promises from God's Word.

The Bible also contains the battle plan for our success. It is a very positive book. Where did we get our negative thinking, our loser mentality? Most of it came from the Church. Many of us have been taught that it's normal for us to sin a little every day, and that it's a major miracle if we can live holy for an entire week. We've been taught to sit quietly in a corner and not say a word. We've adopted the ostrich mentality which says that if we stick our heads in the sand and ignore our problems, they will go away. Or we've assumed the monastery position which locks doors and hides behind them, shutting out the world. That mentality has allowed the Church to be defeated, and that is not God's desire for His people.

We have grown up with concepts about ourselves which are nothing but lies. Some parents have taught their children that they're no good or not important. Some people were taught that the only way to cope with stress is through the bottle. Others were convinced that the only way to get through the day was to pop a pill or shoot up with drugs. Some people were brought up to believe that the only way to resolve their problems was to beat their spouse or abuse their children. But all of those things are lies. The Bible says:

> *Therefore if any man be in Christ, he is a new creature: old things are passed away; behold, all things are become new.*   2 Corinthians 5:17

We can become victorious through a new life in Christ Jesus. We can become more than conquerors through Him.

We *will* have battles because when you decide to go where God wants you to go and do what God wants you to do, the winds of adversity straight from hell itself will begin to blow against you. The winds of this world's system will be contrary to you.

The winds of philosophy and of this world's religious system will all buffet you.

When you begin to press in and possess all that God says you can have, certain elements of society, and even certain elements of the Church, will not embrace you. Instead, they will despise you — because of your blessings.

Those who move to take possession will have many trials. The Bible doesn't hide that fact. But it says that you need not be defeated by any of them. God is with you and will fight for you. He will not do everything for you. He has left it to you to enter in and possess your Promised Land. But you will never be alone. He will always be by your side.

Some people are satisfied with just enough to get them through. I never understood that. It's like sitting down to a Thanksgiving dinner with the juicy turkey, corn bread dressing, mashed potatoes and gravy, glazed carrots, sweet potatoes, and pecan pie and refusing to have more than one item. "Just give me one little slice of dark meat, please, with no gravy." Unbelievable!

For some reason, God's people have believed the lie that they cannot have the fullness and the abundance of what God has promised them. However, God wants us to feast on it all.

There is much that depends on you. You must rise to the challenge and be willing to pay the price for victory. You must be willing to step out of your comfort zone and quit living off yesterday's manna. You must face the adversities, the giants in the land, and look expectantly toward your reward of milk and honey. You must refuse to go back to where you came from, and be determined to go onward with God toward ever greater victories. You must refuse to be held back by religious tradition, prejudice, economic status, sin, or personality conflicts. You must take the necessary steps of faith, sow the necessary seeds of victory, and declare:

> "I'm not afraid of the giants in the land. I'm going to win, whether or not I'm educated, even if my daddy was a con man, no matter if I had a tough childhood, and in spite of the color of my skin. I'm going to march forth and be everything that God created me to be."

We are standing on the brink of the greatest victory the Church has ever seen. But we have some hard choices to make. We must declare, like Joshua, *"But as for me and my house, we will serve the* Lord.*"* We must choose to be children of Almighty God. We must choose to be joint heirs with Jesus Christ. We must choose to be all that God has created us to be. We must choose to be the light of the world and the salt of the earth. We must choose to be that royal priesthood, that holy nation, and that peculiar people.

We must get out of the "maintenance mentality" and get into the possessing position. We must leave behind the fear and the frustration, cut away the

flesh, circumcise our hearts, remember God's goodness and miracles, pray and fast, quit murmuring
and complaining, obey the voice of the Spirit, be
faithful, be militant; and soon the glory of God will
explode upon us, and the giants in the land will fall
before us.

We are about to capture the kings and their mighty
men of valor. We are about to drive out the enemies
from before us. We are about to rise up in God and
take our Promised Land because we are determined
to possess our prophetic promises.